DYKE II

THE DECADENT '90S

ELAINA MARTIN

For Miss Carole Larouche

CONTENTS

AUTHOR'S NOTE

Disclaimer + Content Warning: This memoir deals with drug and alcohol addiction, smoking, nudity, profanity, sex, homophobia, and other possible triggers.

I acknowledge that I work and live on unceded Algonquin land.

Much of this book comes from my memory. For events and details for which I was not present, I relied on conversations and interviews. I have also reconstructed some dialogue according to what I remember and what others have told me. Where dialogue does appear, my intention was to recreate the overall spirit of the conversation rather than provide exact wording. To maintain anonymity, I have changed the names of some people, as well as some of their identifying details. I have also changed the names of some places and organizations, to protect privacy.

With this, the second book in the Dyke series, I wanted to give you a glimpse into what my world looked like during what I refer to as "the decadent nineties." It was a glorious time to be gay in Canada, but it was also a time of deep shifting and opening as a community.

At the beginning of this book, when I am in Sudbury and just freshly out of the closet, you'll see some of my struggles to be my butch self while also attempting to be safe. It was a dangerous time for queer people, especially in Sudbury, a blue-collar mining town whose denizens were mostly uneducated, white, and racist.

The era was just on the heels of the AIDS pandemic, and followed decades of serious, overall hatred towards the gay community, and misunderstanding about HIV/AIDS in general. It was a time of fear and sadness for many who were still losing loved ones, and had been for many painful years. And, it was still happening in such an obvious way. It remains important to note that despite decades of research and discourse, these issues still exist today albeit in altered forms.

The communities were also in a weird state of celebration, as well. It was during this time that queer men and women crossed over and started to share and inhabit more of the same public spaces. "Gay" bars were everywhere in Ottawa. When I moved here in 1997, there were eight active, successful queer bars. That was a lot for a small city like Ottawa, even though it's the national capital of Canada. Anyone who has ever visited here, and certainly those who have lived here, knows how small it is.

It was right before the internet would take us all by storm and provide what was once only found in a physical gay space. Now, people no longer need to leave their homes to find other gay people, or to hook up, thanks to websites, apps and social media.

I believe the nineties were a pivotal time for our queer communities. We went, in one decade, from enjoying our heyday to experiencing what felt like a ghost town. In recent years, there have been no more than three gay bars open here at any one time. I believe Ottawa is down to two right now, both quiet and struggling.

Gay bars and three-storey queer establishments are now a thing of the past in Ottawa. But, because you couldn't all be there, I thought I'd give you a peek at a time gone by, a precious time in queer history in Canada that I'm so happy I got to experience.

Starting in the Big Nickel and heading all the way to Ottawa, I hope you enjoy this look at queerness in the nineties, through this butch Dyke's perspective.

Please stay safe and be good to each other. My many thanks for buying this book, and for your ongoing support.

1

PATSY CLINE

After coming out as queer to just about everyone while I was at Cambrian College in Sudbury doing the Correctional Services Degree Program, I was anxious to find more gay people. It didn't take long.

I met my first other lesbian only a few weeks after my big announcement. She also went to Cambrian. I saw her in the lunchroom. She looked just like k.d. lang, and I know I sound like one of those straight people who think every lesbian either looks like k.d. lang or Ellen DeGeneres, but it's true; she did. I was enamored with k.d. lang at the time, so she easily caught my eye. I guess I checked her out a bit hard, and she smiled.

"Hi," she said, looking directly at me.

I introduced myself and she invited me to sit down. I sat with her and we started talking. She told me her name was Terry. She was very out about her orientation. I was immediately taken aback by her openness, but also thrilled. She was showing me that you could be openly gay, with the right people. We chatted for quite a bit that day. In fact, I skipped my next class to keep speaking with her in the lunchroom during the next period.

We talked about so many things. I mentioned to her that I had come out only a couple of weeks prior and didn't have many gay friends yet, but that I desperately wanted some. She immediately invited me to come over to her apartment later that night to hang out, meet her girlfriend, Shell, and have pizza with them. They always did Pizza Mondays, Terry said, where they ordered pizza in from Topper's, the iconic Sudbury pizza joint. I thought that was cool and accepted her invitation.

It was the first time that, after classes, I didn't head to the Cambrian College residence with my classmates. That was a routine I'd had for over a year. I went to school with them, and headed home with them afterwards. But, they were all straight, and now I was looking for my people. I remember my buddy Rachel being confused, and interested in what I was up to. I told her, that I found a lesbian at the school and I was going to hang out with her. She smiled but I could tell she was jealous.

Terry had invited me to come over at seven p.m. She had given me her address before we said goodbye in the lunchroom. She lived in the Donovan, and I knew exactly where that was. I didn't know yet to bring something with me when I visited someone, so I didn't bring anything, except my guitar. Doing so made both Terry and Shell very happy though.

A little later, I would learn that etiquette is to never visit someone without bringing either food or drink. It's lovely to share both of those things with other humans, and I've become accustom to the ritual. But, like I said, I wasn't there yet that evening.

When I arrived, Shell answered the door. She had the biggest, brightest smile on her face, with bright, merry eyes. She was a big woman, and smiled squinting as she saw me. I was happy to see her, too. It was instantly affirming for me: she was gay, she was a big woman, and she was in a relationship with a small woman. That might not seem like much of a concern, but for me at the time, it was huge. I had all kinds of insecurities about being fat. Meeting Shell instantly made me feel good.

"Hi there. I'm Shell. You must be Elaina. Terry has told me so much about you. Won't you come in?"

"Hi Shell. Thanks so much. Yeah, Terry mentioned she had a beauty at home, as well. It's so nice to come over and hang with my very first lesbians."

"Really?" she laughed. "Well, I'm even more thrilled to meet you then, Elaina."

Terry came from another room, and right away walked over and hugged me.

"Elaina, I'm so happy you came."

"Uh, yeah. I brought my guitar. I hope you don't mind?" That was when Shell squealed.

"Mind?" she laughed. "I love it. Play something for us?"

Terry set down a glass of wine for me. I wasn't used to drinking wine. I'll admit, I was a beer drinker and hated the taste of wine. But I said thanks, and started opening my guitar case.

"Terry tells me you're taking corrections," Shell said. "That's so cool. Do you like the program?"

"I do. I like it. I think I'll be a great CO."

I picked my guitar up out of its case, swung it around my back, and started to tune the strings a bit.

"What kind of music do you like?" I asked them.

They looked at each other and shared a smile, then looked over at me.

"Whatever music you play," Terry said.

I thought that was kind. I laughed.

"Well, how about a little Patsy Cline, then?"

I started playing and singing *Walkin' After Midnight*, a classic Patsy song. I was totally into Patsy Cline, because k.d. lang was into her, and I loved k.d. She had even named her band The Reclines, after Patsy.

k.d. had sung a bunch of Patsy songs on different television episodes I'd seen her on. Her latest cassette tape, which I had just bought and was thoroughly obsessed with, was called *Shadowland*. It was my favourite music at that moment. I played it a hundred times a day. Although k.d. lang hadn't put any Patsy Cline songs on the tape, she had used Cline's producer Owen Bradley for the recordings. That had me buying every Patsy Cline cassette I could find and falling hard for the country starlet.

"I go a walkin', after midnight ...."

I stared to sing and both girls' eyes were on me. Shell's smile was broad, and her eyes were twinkling at me. It was nice. When I was done, Shell couldn't stop herself.

"Oh, Elaina, what a joy you are," she said. "Terry, you didn't tell me Elaina was such a great singer."

"Shell, I only met Elaina today!"

We all laughed. I drank my wine. It was growing on me more with each warm sip.

That night, it turned out to be mostly Shell and I who hung out. Terry was there, but seemed distracted—not rude or anything, but like she was leaving Shell and I to do all the talking. She even got up and went out for a bit. She came back with a laundry hamper under her arm.

"Do you have a laundry room?" I asked Terry when she came back in the door. I had come over to visit with her, and was confused as to why she was doing all this other stuff and not visiting like Shell and I were.

"Yeah. We wash our clothes in the basement. There are a couple of machines down there. It's fairly-cheap. Fifty cents to wash and a quarter to dry."

Just then, there was banging on the door. It was loud and all three of us jumped.

"Hey, let me in, Dykes!" called a voice from the other side of the door.

"Haha! Its Smokey. Let her in, Terry," said Shell.

Terry walked over and opened the door, and this Dyke came in. She was full of energy, hugging and greeting both the girls, when she saw me.

"Who's the big butch?" she asked looking at me.

That made me smile.

"Hi," I said. "I'm Elaina. I'm a friend of Terry's from Cambrian."

"I'm Treena River," she said, "but my friends all call me Smokey."

"I like that name a lot, Smokey" I said. I shook her hand.

"You play guitar? I love the guitar. Can you play me a song?"

Smokey went over to the kitchen, poured herself a glass of wine, and came and sat beside me on the couch. Shell was seated across from us on a big lazy boy chair, and Terry was still standing at the kitchen counter, folding clothes.

"How about this one?" I said. I played an old song I used to hear my grandparents sing, called *For the Good Times*, that I loved singing.

Smokey howled when I finished.

"My dad used to sing that song when I was a kid. That was awesome, bud. Play another?"

So, I did. I played about three more songs. We all laughed in between, with stories Smokey told us about each song I played. She seemed to have a connection to each one. It was so fun.

Smokey was a small woman, but with a huge personality. She was tough, too, I could tell. It was visible on her face, which was full of scars. I immediately felt comfortable with her.

Smokey looked at Terry and then at me.

"Did you want to smoke a joint with us?" she asked.

I started to laugh.

"Um, yes, I do. I have a joint in my pocket, but I wasn't sure if Terry was into it, so I didn't bring it out."

"Oh, I'm into it," said Terry. "But Shell has asthma, so we need to smoke outside.",

"That's not a problem," I said as I started putting on my shoes.

The three of us went outside, around the back of the apartment building, next to the parking lot. The moon was high above us that night. It was late fall and the crisp air felt good. I've always loved the time of year around Halloween. The weather is so vibrant, and everything feels like it's in transition. I felt that way, too.

Smokey asked Terry if she'd be playing this week. That got my attention.

"Playing what?" I asked.

"We play ball in an all-women's league," Smokey explained. "Our team is called The Right Stuff, and we play every Thursday night. Then we go to The Plaza for beers. The season is just finishing up."

"Oh my god. I haven't played ball since I was a kid, but I love it so much"

"Are you joking?" Smokey was acting very serious now.

"No, not at all. I played a lot of ball when I was a kid, my dad taught me lots, because he played in a regular blooper ball league and I was their batgirl."

"Holy shit. Terry, you hearing this?" Terry grinned at Smokey.

"Are you free this coming Thursday at six p.m. to come meet the girls and have a practice with us? Although our season is just finishing up, we need more girls. And *you*? Well, you'd be perfect."

Smokey looked me up and down. Then she started to laugh.

"Oh, shit. I'm going to be a fucking hero!"

Smokey couldn't stop patting herself on the back. I was thrilled, too. I wanted to play ball again.

"We're playing at the Terry Fox field Thursday. You know where that is?" she asked.

I did remember it. It was a big stadium with multiple fields that I'd played at years before, as a kid.

"I do, and I'll see you there. Thanks for the invite, Smokey."

"This is so great Elaina," said Terry. "I'm so glad you stopped by, Smokey."

We had continued walking around the apartment to the front door, as we were done our joints. We headed back inside. I was feeling overjoyed about meeting Shell, and visiting with Terry, and now having met the incredible Smokey.

It was getting late, nearing ten o'clock. I had classes tomorrow and so did Terry. I was thinking I should probably get going. I got up and started to put my guitar away.

"You're not going already?" asked Shell.

"Yeah, I think I must. I have school tomorrow. Do you have class tomorrow, Terry?"

She looked over at me.

"I do, Elaina. Maybe catch you in the lunchroom?"

"I can't wait," I said. "It was so amazing of you both to have me over. Thank you. Hey, Smokey. It was awesome to meet you, too. I can't wait to see you Thursday."

"Thank you for coming, Elaina," said Shell, popping up from her chair. "I'm so happy I got to meet you and hear your voice. Come back again soon, 'kay?"

Shell held her arms up. She was a big girl, but also very short. I had to lean right over to accept her lengthy hug. She was full of warmth.

"Thanks, Shell. You're the sweetest." I gave her a little kiss on the cheek while she squeezed the shit out of me.

"Yes. Thanks for coming, Elaina," said Terry. "I'll see you tomorrow?"

"I'll do my best to find you and we can go for a smoke between class or something. Thanks for having me over, and for introducing me to your amazing Shell."

"Great to meet you Elaina!" Smokey piped up.

"It was so great to meet you too, Smokey."

We hugged extra-long. It had been nice to visit with Terry and to meet Shell. She was incredibly sweet. But meeting Smokey, and being invited to play ball with a bunch of women? Gay women? Wow. That was everything. I floated to my car.

I got in and headed back to Coniston. I was staying at my parents' place, in their basement in a bedroom under the stairs, with a large, open rec room all to myself, while I finished college. I wasn't there much, though, since I was always going to the Cambrian student residence with my classmates. But it was where I was headed this night.

While driving, I was thinking about Terry and Shell, and how sweet they both were. I considered how distracted Terry had looked, way more so than she had when we were speaking earlier in the day at school. Also, there was Smokey and this coming Thursday. I was full of anticipation, and scared shitless, honestly.

So many thoughts were going through my mind. I couldn't wait to get home, lay in bed, and think about it all. Thursday couldn't come fast enough.

2

LEZ PLAY BALL

Sitting in the lunchroom at Cambrian on Tuesday, I was telling all my classmates around the table about meeting the girls, Terry and Shell.

I was ecstatic to be hanging out with my first, real lesbian friends. My buddies listened and nodded with smiles while I told them everything that had happened. I mentioned being invited to the ball practice on Thursday after school, and how excited I was.

"That's two nights this week you're hanging with them?" Rachel piped up.

"Yes. And I can't wait!"

Rachel rolled her eyes and groaned. I didn't remark. I knew she was just jealous, pouting, and pissed that I wasn't driving them home to the residence and partying all night like we usually did on a Thursday. I didn't say anything. I loved Rachel and didn't want to fight with her, so I ignored her outburst.

When classes finished on Thursday, instead of piling as many friends as I could fit into my big car and heading to the residence, I got in my car alone and went to Coniston so I could shower and get into my ball gear to head over to the Terry Fox complex for the Dyke practice. I was nervous, but also eager for them to see how well I played ball.

Rachel called just as I had gotten out of the shower. I answered the phone because I was walking by the bar in the basement where the phone was.

"Hello?"

"Hey, pal. What you doing?"

"Aww, you miss me?"

"Yes. We all do. Who's going to go get the booze tonight?"

"Haha. You'll have to figure that out, sweetie."

"I'm just joking. Just wanted to wish you luck, and tell you that I miss ya."

"That's sweet, Rachel. Thanks. I'm so excited. I'm just off to get dressed and head out."

"If your practice doesn't go too late, will you come by afterwards?"

"For sure I will."

"Yay, okay. We'll see you later then!"

Rachel said goodbye and sounded happy enough by the time we hung up. I continued to my room to get dressed and head out.

I was upstairs grabbing a glass of water and bumped into my dad, so I told him about my ball practice. He was shocked I was playing ball, and a smile came over his face, which made me happy.

I didn't get into who I was playing with, though, because my dad was still a bit weirded out by my having come out as gay. He loved me, but he was quiet now with me. It was much harder to speak with him. He seemed to avoid me now. I think he was worried I was different. Of course, I wasn't. I just needed to give him some time to see that, and I was.

I was patient with my dad, because he was so soft-mannered and kind, even though he'd lost that sparkle in his eye with me. I continued to hope it would come back.

I drove to Sudbury, taking the Kingsway into town, since that was the quickest route to the Lasalle bypass where the Terry Fox field was. I was nervous thinking about who I would meet, and how I would show them my strengths at throwing a ball, how I wasn't afraid of the ball, how well I could play infield, and all my little ball-playing tricks. Hell, I couldn't wait to just throw a ball with someone. It had been years.

When I got to the complex, I drove into the parking lot and, to my surprise, saw what looked like thousands of lesbians in the lot. I would find out later that they weren't all lesbians, but I'll tell you, women in ball gear look like Dykes to me.

There were women getting out of their cars all over, or carrying their ball bags up the trails to the separate ball fields. I saw so many women, it was exhilarating. I had to be careful not to drive into someone as I pulled in, because I was terribly distracted.

I parked and hopped out. I grabbed my glove and ball bag and started to look for Terry or Smokey. It was a sea of women, all headed to three different ball fields. Those ball fields already had women on them, as well.

I was overwhelmed, still excited but a little nervous now that I had to walk around and look for two people who I didn't know overly well, in this sea of women. I kept looking for jerseys that said "The Right Stuff" on the women walking around, hoping I would spot someone from the team.

Then, suddenly, I was jumped from behind. It nearly knocked me over, but I stood strong and carried my new rider. It was Smokey.

She had seen me from the parking lot and had been running to catch up, then jump me from behind, which she did.

I was twisting, trying to figure out which old friend was on me, and laughing when I realized it was Smokey. When she got down, she had her giant smile on, and big, loving eyes, and was laughing hard. I instantly adored Smokey. She brought me to the field where The Right Stuff women's team was practicing.

Smokey immediately started introducing me to everyone. It was going to be difficult to remember all the names, I thought. But I listened intently.

"This is Dart." Smokey pointed at a larger woman.

"Hey," Dart replied.

"Silver, meet Elaina."

"Hey," Silver replied.

"Polly, this is Elaina."

"Hi. Welcome," said Polly.

It went on and on down the bench and over to the lineup at the fence of women getting their gear on and starting to toss a ball. I was now wondering; do lesbians all have funny names?

I met Carole, Cody, Mags, Cindy, Shoddy, and the list of intros continued. Smokey was so kind and took me under her wing.

When Terry finally showed up, she looked rough. It was nice to see her, though. I went over right away when she walked into the diamond, to say "Hi" to her.

"Hey, Terry," I said. "This is so great. Thanks for asking me out here tonight with you and Smokey. She's already introduced me to half the team."

"That's great, bud."

Again, though, Terry looked distracted, like she had the other night at her place, not like when we first met in the lunchroom and she was so engaging and talkative and open, all bright and positive. Now, she was all doom and gloom.

"What's up, bud? You okay?" I asked her.

"Oh yeah. Just dealing with something."

"The Right Stuff?" She looked at me, confused. I laughed and said, "You know. The team name?" Then she laughed with me.

"Okay," I said. "Well, please let me know if I can help in any way?"

"I will. Thanks, Elaina"

She looked at me then. Her eyes closed slightly and she smiled at me. There was something off with her, for sure. I could see it. The eyes never lie.

Smokey came and asked me to throw a ball with her. All the girls were teaming up in twos to throw a ball and warm their arms up for play.

I was thrilled to play catch with Smokey. I tested her out with a couple of easy throws, to see her catching ability, before I started driving them over. She was good. She could handle each throw, and each one I gave was harder. I whipped one over so hard it took her off her feet when she caught it. But she did catch it. Then she yelped out loud and threw her glove and the ball both on the ground. She was jumping up and down, waving one hand in the air.

"Damn, Dyke," she called. "That's a mighty arm you have. Did you ladies see that? She nearly took me down with that throw."

The women started laughing and I thought it was a great icebreaker. Smokey was bragging to everyone about finding me. She was immediately my person. We just connected, like we had when we first met at Terry and Shell's on Monday night. Smokey and I would continue to be fast friends from there. She was fun and hilarious, too, with a sense of humour I could get behind, raw and silly and totally over the top.

Smokey would sit beside me on the bench, run out into the field with me, keep introducing me to other women. She didn't leave my side.

The Dyke who coached the team, Lorna, put most of the girls out in the field and we started batting practice. One at a time, she'd call the women over to take the bat. Lorna stood throwing balls at each of them, and they hit the balls out into the field as hard as they could.

I was out there with Smokey and she was giving me the play by play on each Dyke as they went up to bat. Smokey was cracking me up with her anecdotes on each player as they hit the balls, or didn't. She told me stories showing how they either sucked or rocked at hitting, plus whatever else came out of her about them. She was hilarious. And I was instantly learning a lot about these women. I liked this game of Smokey's. Then she said, "Watch this."

I looked over at the plate and it was a woman she had introduced me to earlier, named Carole. She was a French woman and everyone said her name with a French accent, like Ca-rawl. I liked that, as I've always had an affinity for accents.

She held the bat like she could swing it. She was a large-busted woman, and I wasn't sure how fast she would run the bags. But, hey, if you can hit the ball hard enough, you can walk the bags— that was always my mantra, anyway. Being fat, I was always way slower than others, but, in this case, bigger meant stronger, and that comes in handy when hitting the ball.

Carole cracked each ball that was thrown at her, even the shitty throws. She didn't miss a ball. She'd run up to hit a ball that was delivered short. She'd step back from the plate to crack one totally inside. You could tell she just loved to hit the ball. She'd crack them left field. She'd crack them right field. She'd hit them low and drive them up the centre of the infield between first and second base. And she'd do the same between the second and third bases. She could literally place the ball anywhere she wanted. She was that good.

I was in awe…and Smokey watched me stand there drooling over Carole, I had never seen a woman hit the ball like her before.

"Wow!" That's all I could say.

Smokey and I were pretty much standing shoulder to shoulder out there, talking. I guess Carole wanted to break up the party, because we suddenly heard a woman yell, "Right field!"

That was the coach shouting. She could see we weren't watching, too busy laughing and horsing around, and Carole had hit the ball so hard it was headed right for us.

But, I put my glove up and caught the ball without having to make one step. Smokey and I were shocked, and it had startled us out of our wits. That had been Carole's plan all along. She was standing at home plate, doubled over she was laughing so hard. Stunned, Smokey and I looked at each other, then at the coach, who was now also buckled over laughing, and then at Carole. And we all started laughing, too. The entire field of women was laughing, and I knew, I just knew then, that these women were my new people.

Carole had played us. She saw us having a good time out there and decided to send a ball right to us, knowing she could place one anywhere. It was a good joke. We started hollering.

"Haha! Nice one, ladies," Smokey yelled out.

"You got us," I cried.

We all laughed more, then continued to practice. When it was my turn at the bat, I swung and swung. I kept missing the ball. A Dyke behind me at the plate, being catcher for this practice, was calling," Saaa-wing batta batta, an-a miss," each time. I wanted to shove my fucking bat down her throat. But I smiled and giggled. I knew she was joking. But it was starting to piss me off. I knew if I only connected, I would show her.

It had been a while since I had swung a bat, and I had been nervous to begin with. The more I missed the ball, the more nervous I got. Standing there, I was thinking so many things, all negative, of course, like that they weren't going to want me, that I sucked, that they were going to think I was just a fat Dyke who couldn't play, that they were going to laugh at me.

Just then, a ball came at me so perfectly I could see it arriving straight from the pitcher's mound, at a perfect waist height, right in my sweet spot, right where I liked it, and I pulled my inside leg towards my back leg and stepped into my swing like it was my last swing on Earth. And holy Christ it connected. Crack!

The ball went high up and far out. The girls all started howling. They were all watching the ball. I was watching my ball. It kept going and going. Smokey was screaming from left field. I just stood there watching, and the smile on my face got larger and larger. That ball left the field and landed on another field in play, behind ours.

All the women roared. The one playing catcher shouted, "Now, that's what I was waiting for. I knew you had it in ya," and I forgave her for her earlier taunting.

Smokey ran over and yelled at the other team on the other field to throw her the ball back.

"Sorry! We've got our own Barry Bonds over here."

Everyone laughed. Even the girls from the other field were all looking over and laughing. Our coach walked over to me.

"Okay, well, if you're gonna hit like that when you do connect, the strikes will work themselves out," she said.

I was pleased with that. Some of the girls ran over to high five me and tap my bum for the great hit. I was happy they at least got to see what I could do when I did connect with the ball. I just had to connect that once. I was overjoyed that I'd done it for all of them to see.

The practice continued to be loads of fun. We finished up around nine. It was dark, but the lights had all come on by the fields at around eight. It was so fun to be out with all these Dykes playing ball. I felt a warmth and happiness that I couldn't remember feeling before. I looked up at the sky, which was turning colours, and around me at all the women, many of them standing in the dim spots between the stadium lights, and I just breathed.

Smokey came and plopped down beside me on the bench while I was packing my shit into my ball bag. She was already packed up and ready to head out.

"I sure hope you're coming for drinks, pal," she said. "It's the best part of practice."

"I'm supposed to head to the res and have drinks with my class."

"But we're more fun," Smokey laughed. She was right. Not that they were more fun, exactly. But, if I could only explain what it felt like to be with women who were like me. Some were way Dykier than me, even. I felt so at home, it was reassuring and welcoming and perfect.

As I looked at all the women walking to their cars from the three different fields, I asked Smokey, "Are those all lesbians?"

She laughed.

"I, wish! The only Dyke team is ours, The Right Stuff. Those other teams are all straight women. But they're cool with us."

"Oh, wow. Okay. Do you think the team liked me, Smokey?"

"I think you'll have to come drinking with us to seal the deal, pal!" She winked at me.

"Okay, I'm coming," I laughed. "You got me."

Smokey said she'd come with me in my car so she could show me where they all went for drinks after each game. It was an old, raggedy place on Howey Drive, and it backed onto Minnow Lake. It was quite far from the fields, but I guess a team of Dykes had to be particular about where they hang out.

The bar was called the Plaza Hotel. I had seen it the many times I had driven by there. I used to work at a Petro-Canada gas station down the street. It was an area I was very familiar with, although I had never been to this bar before. Turned out that a lot of the Dykes lived around there, including Smokey, so it was close to home for most of them.

We parked in the lot that wrapped around the building. Smokey asked me if I wanted to smoke a joint. Of course, I said yes.

We stood by the side of the building, in the parking lot, smoking our joint, and watched as all the girls pulled up. We had gotten there first, chatting the entire time. I'm a pretty fast driver, so there we were, greeting the team. We teased or talked to each woman who showed up as they went by us.

Smokey and I were like two peas in a pod from the get-go; we just got each other. It was like we had been friends for decades, like we already understood each other, even knew what the other was thinking. We finished our joint and went inside.

The women were playing pool, or sitting at little, round tables, clinking their beers and talking loudly. It was a beautiful sight to me. I was elated. Smokey asked me to play pool. I went over to the table and put my quarter on the side, behind a few other quarters already sitting there, to show my intent and get in line to play.

Smokey and I sat down with Carole and Cindy at their table. That turned out to be a great decision. Not only had Carole fooled us both out on the field earlier by sending that cracker ball right to us, she was a hoot all the time. That evening, we laughed until we cried. Carole was wonderfully animated and, between her and Smokey, my stomach got sore from laughing. I was having so much fun. Smokey and Carole were talking about women they knew, and telling funny stories. Then Smokey looked over at the table next to us and asked someone there, "Are you still having us all over tomorrow night?"

Another ball player from our team, Cathy, replied, "I sure am. Julie is coming and bringing her guitar. We'll be playing a bit."

"Girls and guitars. Sounds fun to me," I replied.

"Cathy," said Smokey. "I heard Elaina play at Terry's earlier this week, and she is really good. You've gotta hear her."

"Can you bring your guitar and come by, Elaina?"

I was nervous. I didn't know what to say, but I was also happy she had asked me.

"Yeah, I'll see. I've got plans with my class, but I'll see what I can do."

Smokey and I decided to go outside to smoke another joint at one point. On our way out, we saw Terry on the payphone down a hallway near the washrooms with her back to us. Smokey and I looked at each other. She put her index finger up in front of her mouth and winked at me. I caught her drift right away. We snuck over to Terry, bent over, and creeped slowly down the hall, so as to pop up and scare her. It would be funny, for us and for Shell, who we figured Terry was on the phone with.

Once we were halfway we could hear that Terry was on the phone, alright, but she was half-whispering. We stopped.

"Cindy," we heard her say. "I love you. Don't be like that."

Smokey looked back at me. I was still bent in half. My eyes widened as I looked at her. We both turned and crept back out from where we were. On our tiptoes, we ran to the door and jumped outside and pulled out our joint. We were all nervous, confused and still wide-eyed.

"What was that?" I asked Smokey.

"Fuck. I don't know, chum." Some other girls came out of the bar and we started laughing, pretending we'd just told each other another joke, which we were constantly doing anyway.

We ended up staying at the bar until it closed at two a.m. We were all drunk and content. Smokey told me to stay at her place, which was just down the street. She said Mags would drop us off, and I could pick up my Jeep tomorrow morning. I agreed. I was having so much fun I didn't want to go home to Coniston, or back to school. I just wanted to stay with these Dykes forever, be with them for the rest of my life.

Smokey did only live a few blocks away. When we got into her apartment, we smoked one last joint. Then she threw me a pillow and blanket, and I passed out hard on her couch. Her girlfriend Tracey woke me up in the morning.

"Sorry! Sorry, sorry," someone said.

I was groggy and severely hungover, but I could hear a woman apologizing. Then the blender started and I thought my head was going to pop off. It was Tracey, Smokey's girlfriend. It was only six a.m., but she worked at the Sudbury General Hospital and had to get out the door to catch her bus there.

I woke and sat up.

"Hi. I'm Elaina," I said. "Smokey took me …."

Tracey cut me off, saying she knew. Smokey had filled her in. Nick said it was nice to meet me.

"Hopefully, we'll have time to get to know each other in the future," she said, "but I have to go to work."

She was gone. Smokey had woken up when she'd heard us talking. She came and sat on the couch beside me. She grabbed the TV remote and turned it on.

"What's your schedule today, bud? Wanna hang out?" she asked.

"Oh, my goodness. Fuck yeah, I do."

I had class, but I wasn't going to not stay with Smokey. She'd made me feel great, had me over, and introduced me to everyone. She was my new best friend. I could tell we were bonding. I wanted to stay.

"Can I use your phone for a second?" I asked.

"Sure, bud. It's in the kitchen." I walked over and called Rachel. I knew she would still be at the residence, but awake, since the residence crowd had to catch a bus at around seven-thirty in the morning when I wasn't there to drive them.

"Hello?"

"Hey, bud. It's me."

"Elaina? Where were you last night? I waited all night for you."

"I know. I'm sorry, sweetie. I got caught up with stuff. I'm taking care of some family business today, so I won't be in class. Can you let everyone know for me? I'll be back on Monday. Can you grab me some notes?"

"Okay, but won't I see you tonight?"

"Of course. It's Friday night, baby!"

"Okay, great. Perfect. I'll see you tonight, then. Good luck with your family business today." She sounded funny at that, like she knew I was lying and didn't have family business. Or maybe that was just me, since lying is something that always stresses me out. I hate lying; it causes all kinds of issues, and the truth always comes out, and then you're completely fucked. Also, I have a terrible memory, probably from years of pot smoking, I know. But, it's good to be realistic about these things. I just try not to lie. It's less work.

We hung up and I went back to sit with Smokey on the couch. We rolled joints and talked and talked. We spent the day being silly. Smokey made me pancakes, then we went for a walk to get smokes at the store.

The Mac's Milk was on the other side of Minnow Lake, so we got to walk around the lake that morning, which was beautiful, and the walk felt good. Smokey told me stories of Dykes and other people she knew in town, and I told her about growing up in Coniston and some of my shit. We went over to the Plaza Hotel and got my car, and I drove Smokey home.

It was going on noon and I thought I'd taken up enough of Smokey's time.

"I should get going, bud," I said. "I'm sure you have shit to do."

"I don't," she said. "Please stay. We'll hang out and you can have dinner with me and Tracey when she gets home, and then come to Cathy's party with us tonight."

"Oh, shit!" I had forgotten all about that. But I was delighted remembering and thinking about it. "I said I'd bring my guitar, and it's out in Coniston. I also need to change. I'm still in my ball clothes."

"I'll go with you. It'll be fun. I haven't been out to Coniston in years."

We started the drive out to my parents' place, talking the entire time. I showed Smokey where I had hung out as a kid and teenager, and where my friends from high school lived. I pointed out where Margie, my best friend from high school, lived. I told Smokey how I'd had a falling out with Margie, and why we weren't friends anymore, which was still a raw sore spot for me.

When we got to my folks' place and went inside, the place was empty. No one was home. We went into my basement and Smokey looked around while I packed my bag and got my guitar. I asked her if she would mind if I took a quick shower, and she said to take my time. I told her to look around and make herself at home.

When I was done my shower, we went up to the kitchen and I fried us up some leftover spaghetti I found in the fridge. I guess that's what my parents had eaten for dinner the previous night. It was great, and we ate our spaghetti and laughed and sat around looking at my parents' photos on the walls. I told Smokey about my plan to be a correctional officer and, most recently, about finding my gay self.

She was such a good listener and had great advice. When I told her about my dad, and mentioned the hard time he was having with me coming out gay, Smokey put her hand on my shoulder and looked me in the eyes.

"He loves you," she said. "He'll come around. Just try to be patient."

She was right.

3
___

MISS ELAINEOUS

Smokey and I hung out in Coniston all day. We were having fun at my folks' place, and then my mother came home. She was being all friendly and sweet and joking around, so that made Smokey laugh.

When we were leaving, Smokey said, "Your mom's the coolest. She's so funny. You're lucky!"

"Don't be fooled, friend," I replied. "She's a demon under that smile."

Smokey laughed like I was making another joke, but I didn't laugh. I left it where it was, though. I didn't feel like ruining our good time explaining all the cruel things that my mother had done and said to everyone in my family going as long back as I could remember. Or what she had done to me when I was five when my Aunt's brother raped me in my aunt's downstairs bathroom. And my mother did nothing about it when she found out—except yell at me, and blame me, a five-year-old kid, for not having screamed when it happened. She even continued to bring me back to the house where it had happened, where I would have to use the only bathroom in their house, the bathroom I had been raped in. I had to go there hundreds of times over the years, over and over again. I wasn't going to get into all of that now.

It was five-thirty by the time we were walking out the back door to the alley with the driveway behind my folks' house. My dad was pulling in with his new truck. He smiled when he saw me, but, when he saw Smokey with me, his smile turned, right before my eyes. I saw it.

We waited, because I wanted to say hi to my dad. Plus, I wanted to borrow his cooler. When he climbed out of his truck, I went over and hugged him. I told him we were off to party with the ball team I was now on. I asked if I could borrow his beer cooler for the night. I figured introducing him to Smokey by saying she was on the ball team would make him happy. And it did. He was smiling again.

"Yes. Just please be sure to bring it back clean," he said.

"Stay safe out there, girls."

"We will. Thanks, Dad. Love you."

"I love you, too."

My dad couldn't have more of a relationship with me right now, because he was going through his own revelations about queerness, and was coming to terms with my recent coming out. But he loved me, and he made subtle attempts like this to show me. I caught each one.

I was also in and out a lot around that time, doing my own thing.

We sped up the old road back into Sudbury, zipping up Bancroft Drive, through the Moonlight Beach area, and up along Minnow Lake, until we hit Howey Drive and pulled into Smokey's place. When we got into her apartment, Tracey was already home and eating her dinner. She looked tired.

"Hey, you two. How was your day?" She looked up, with mac and cheese on her fork, as she asked us.

Smokey jumped in to answer.

"We had a great day. Elaina took me to Coniston, to her folks' place, where she's staying while she's in school. We had spaghetti and I met both of her parents."

"Smokey is amazing, Tracey," I said. "I see why you love her so much. We had a great day. I feel so lucky."

"Nothing lucky about me, kid," Smokey joked.

"You guys think you can go to the party without me tonight?" Tracey asked. She was so tired we could hear it in her voice. Smokey and I looked at each other.

"Is that safe?" Smokey asked.

We all burst out laughing.

"You okay, Tracey?" I asked.

Smokey went over and put her arms around Tracey from behind. She held Tracey close, kissing her neck.

"I'm okay," she said. "I'm just so tired. It's been a real long week at the hospital, and I'm just not up for a party. I'm so happy you're here, Elaina, and that Smokey has a buddy to go with."

"I'll take the best care of your sweetheart for you, Tracey. I promise."

I went over and sat in front of the television, to give them some time together. I got myself into some *The Little Rascals* while the girls hung out and got caught up on Tracey's day.

The phone rang, and Smokey picked it up.

"Hello?"

I could hear someone on the other end of the phone talking a mile a minute, and laughing.

"Yeah, we are. It's me and Elaina. We've been hanging out since last night. Tracey's tired. What time are you heading over?"

Carole was very loud and exuberant. I could hear her through the phone.

"Okay, we'll be there in an hour or so. See you soon, chum."

Carole was making sure Smokey was coming. Carole had mentioned she was glad that I was coming, too. That made me smile.

We hung out with Tracey for another hour or so. We helped her clean up, made her some popcorn, and got her settled in and comfortable on the couch in front of the TV.

"Elaina, feel free to come back here and crash tonight after the party, okay?"

"Thanks, Tracey. That's awesome," I said. "I'll make sure we both get back here safe and sound."

This was, I thought, probably not a promise I should have been making, honestly. Smokey and I packed up our stuff, and were headed over to Cathy's place. But first, we made a quick stop at the beer store to fill the cooler I had borrowed from my dad.

Cathy lived up on Kelly Lake Road, which was close to where my dad worked at the Loeb warehouse on Lorne Street. I knew the Northern Ale brewery was up around there. It was Sudbury's own brewery. My dad would bring it home sometimes when the beer store would go on strike in Sudbury. I thought it would be cool showing up with Sudbury's own beer, Northern Ale. It would be much better than the Molson Canadian every single other Dyke would be drinking, I was sure.

I popped into the sales door of the brewery and got us a two-four. I came back to the car, opened the trunk, and filled the cooler with beer. Now we needed ice.

"Hey, bud," Smokey said. "Let me pitch in for the beer."

She passed me a ten-dollar bill. I chuckled.

"You're putting me up at your place," I said. "The least I can do is get us there and buy the beer, bud." I pushed her money back to her.

"You're the best," she said.

"No, you are!"

We pulled into the Petro-Canada up the street and Smokey jumped out and got two bags of ice. She threw them over our beer in the cooler. We were set. Off to the party.

Cathy's wasn't far from where we were now, only a few streets away. When we arrived, I saw that she lived in a slender, tall house, two stories high, with blue siding. The driveway was wide and long. It was already packed with cars, and it was only seven o'clock. When we parked the car, and got out, we could hear music. Guitars were already playing. I immediately got excited. I walked around to the trunk and pulled my guitar and the cooler out. Smokey grabbed the cooler, and we made our way up to the house.

There were some girls outside, smoking, when we got to the door. Cathy didn't smoke, so any smokers would be smoking outside tonight. That's where the real party would be, I knew.

Smokey introduced me to each woman we passed, and they all greeted Smokey joyfully. I could tell Smokey was someone everyone liked.

When we got inside, there was a circle of women in the living room, four with guitars, and two singing. It was nice and loud. I loved to be entertained, so Smokey and I each grabbed a beer from out of our cooler, leaned against a wall near the players, and caught the show for a bit.

I was thankful that Northern Ale sold cold beer out of their brewery, because our beer wouldn't have had enough time to get cold yet. Smokey and I cracked our beers and clinked them together.

"Cheers," we said.

We slugged our cold beers. She was reminding me that she not only liked beer as much as I did, but our drinking habits were similar. We killed that first beer and opened number two. I smiled and thought to myself that Smokey was my bud, for sure.

Then we heard a howl from the back door. I knew right away it could only be one person: Carole. It was, and she was raring to go. She had a beer already in her hand as she came into the house, and was cracking jokes with everyone as she squeezed through the crowd of lesbians. Everyone knew her here, as well. She walked directly over to us, hugged Smokey, then hugged me tight, pulled back, and held my shoulders.

"I'm so glad you're here," she said.

I'm pretty sure I fell in love with her in that moment. Then, she was off, laughing with this girl and that girl. Everyone knew and seemed to love Carole.

I immediately adored how much laughing I was doing with these new friends. I loved my other friends, too, but they didn't laugh as much. I don't know if it's a gay thing, but I sure loved it.

Smokey and I watched the women play their guitars for a bit, until we decided it was time to smoke a joint. During a break between songs, we asked around to see if anyone wanted to join us. Of course, Carole did, as did Silver, and Terry, who had just shown up and was still standing at the door.

"Hey, Terry! Great to see you." I gave her a quick hug.

"It's great to see you, Elaina," she said. "I'm so happy you're here."

"Me too. I've been hanging with Smokey since ball yesterday, and it's all because of you. Thanks, Terry!"

"You're welcome."

We all went outside. We clinked our beers and passed around two joints and laughed and told jokes, and it was fun to hang with these lesbians. I kept thinking to myself, "Is this the life I am going to live now?" Fuck, I was happy. I couldn't believe I had found my people, just like that, pretty much overnight. I was thrilled and wondered if this could all be real. Fuck it. Glug, glug. I kept drinking.

After we were all pleasantly stoned and getting good and sauced, we went back into the party, which was in full swing. There were lesbians everywhere, and each time we'd pass someone, either Smokey or Carole would introduce them to me. I couldn't remember half the names, but I loved how either one, or even both of them together, would introduce me to every person.

Some of the girls would answer, "Yeah, yeah. We know, we met her last night." They were kind of making a point, like enough already, we've met her.

In a pause between songs, Smokey yelled across the gaggle of women in the circle playing guitars and singing.

"You all need to hear Elaina sing and play," she said. "She's awesome."

"Did you bring your guitar?" Cathy shouted over to me. There were so many women, in that room, the back room, the kitchen, all laughing and talking, no one could hear anything unless you yelled.

"Yeah. It's right there," I shouted back, and pointed over at my case, which was leaning against the wall.

"Come jam with us," Cathy called as she lifted her right arm off her guitar long enough to wave me over.

I got my guitar out, grabbed my capo and a couple of picks out of my case, and headed over. I found a spot on the floor, leaning against the couch. I was damn nervous, I'll tell you. I hadn't met any of the women in this room yet. None of them had been at the ball practice. These were the artists, not the sporty Dykes.

I also hadn't played for people much at this point. I had mostly been playing for myself since my dad bought me the guitar for Christmas a couple of years ago. He taught me my first three chords. I'd been playing and singing ever since, but that wasn't long at all.

The women were playing an Indigo Girls song and I just followed along, playing the chords I could see the other girls playing, and watching intently. It was fun. I had never played along with other people before. I had also never played any Indigo Girls songs. I was learning quickly that lesbians loved the Indigo Girls. They seemed to play song after song, and most of the women at the party would sing the words to every song, like a choir. It was weird and wild all at once.

There were now five acoustic guitars being played, and most of the women around the circle were singing. They had sung together before, you could tell. They knew the songs and even sang harmony to some of them. That was awesome. I kept playing and Smokey would crack me beers and pass them over, like she was my own personal stage manager. I loved her so much already, and we'd only known each other less than a week.

After a few more songs, the woman leading the group, and doing most of the singing, a very striking lesbian and a bit older than the others, looked at me.

"So, when do we hear this 'great' voice?" she asked.

I wasn't sure at that moment whether she was being nice or not. It was hard to tell from the way she said it and how she looked at me. It made me even more nervous, which I'm pretty sure was what she was attempting to do. I swigged my beer, found my confidence and straightened my back.

"Right now?" I said.

I wanted to wow them. The problem was I only knew Patsy Cline and a few simple k.d. lang songs, and these women had been playing a completely different kind of music all night. This made me nervous, as well. I decided to just do it. Liquid courage often helped in those sticky, anxious situations.

I played *Crazy* by Patsy Cline. And instead of staying seated like all the other women had all night while playing, I got up. I stood with my guitar around myself and started playing and singing, just as I always did at home alone in my basement, with my eyes closed.

"Crazy. I'm crazy for feeling so lonely."

The room got quiet, quieter than I could remember it having been all night. It was just me, my voice, and my guitar. When I opened my eyes, all the lesbians were staring at me, smiling. I continued and sang the entire song, being as brazen as I could with both my playing and the lyrics. It's an easy song, and repetitive, with very few chords and lyrics in general. It was a great song for just that moment. I'd also sung it about a hundred times before.

When I finished the song and bowed my head, the entire house starting yelling and freaking out. They were all coming over and patting my back and saying things like, "Holy shit, you're good. Wow, you're so talented."

It made me feel great. I had never had anyone call me talented before. I just played for fun.

"You're pretty good. But are you a one-trick pony?"

I turned and searched the room for who had said that, and yep, it was the woman who had been leading all the women playing before. She had this strange smile on her face as I looked at her. Everyone was watching, so I think she was acting by smiling, but I knew right away, this one was going to be trouble.

She was obviously not impressed. I assumed it was because she had been used to getting all the attention, being the main singer and player. I guessed she didn't like me stealing her thunder. But hell, that was the last thing I was trying to do. I was just being me.

"Yep, one-trick pony, that's me."

I put my guitar in its case.

"I just want to listen to you sing and play all night," I said.

"You're so good."

I smiled at her, a quick, fake smile, like the one she had given me seconds before. I wanted her to know that I wasn't going to play with her and act like I didn't realize what she was doing. I also knew this was her crowd, and her friends. Plus, I just didn't want to deal with her.

"I just played that song for my new best friend, Smokey. Now we've got some drinking to do," I said. "Have fun, ladies."

I grabbed my guitar case and walked to the door. I figured I might as well put my guitar away in my car while I had it in my hand. I certainly wasn't going to play anymore that night, and this way I left the ladies all wanting to hear more.

That's how I handled it. Smokey and I kept putting beers back one after the other, laughing and listening to the other women playing all night. We'd head outside and smoke joints and cigarettes, then we'd come back in. This went on, back and forth, for hours.

Carole was with us pretty much all night, too. She was very engaging. She was blonde, with the bluest eyes, big breasts, and a hot body, and her laugh was infectious. She was also very intense, and I loved it. She never said anything to you without staring at you deeply, right into your eyes. Everything always seemed meaningful with her because of that.

While we were outside smoking, I had to pee. I'm not sure where I picked up this habit, but I figured I would just find a bush and squat, give a little wiggle to shake the drips, and be done with it. So, that's what I went off to do, because I had to go. Smokey and I had already drunk six beers each. I walked around the house to the back, where I could see a field, a bunch of junk, a garage, and an open, empty lot next to that.

Heading down a path, I stumbled around some garbage bags. Just as I was grabbing my pants to pull them down, I literally bumped into Terry. She was back there in a full-blown necking session with one of the other lesbians I had seen inside earlier. They were making out fiercely when I bumped into them.

Terry twisted her body around in shock. As she looked at me, her eyes practically shot out of her head like she was a cartoon character. Her friend just looked at me a smiled. She looked half-cut.

"Holy shit, bud, you scared me. Uh, what's up?" Terry asked me, all nervous.

"What are *you* doing?" I chuckled nervously.

Terry grabbed me and pulled me close to her, aggressively.

"We need to talk," she said. She was backing me up, around to the other side of the garage. She kind of shoved me and was talking frantically, a mile a minute. I stopped her.

"I have to pee," I said. "Fuck, that's why I'm back here." I crouched down and dropped my pants and pissed right in front of her. It was now urgent.

As I was peeing, I told Terry, "Listen, this is your thing. I don't want anything to do with it."

"Oh?" she said. "Okay, great then. Thanks."

"I just need to piss. It's usually done in private, but …."

I stumbled a bit while getting up and pulling up my drawers, pretending to be drunker than I was. I slurred my words to drive that message home, and Terry seemed pleased with that, like she had convinced herself I was too drunk to remember what I'd seen. She backed off. My plan had worked. I knew exactly what I was doing.

I walked around the garage and started back toward the house. Terry stayed behind with her friend. I was thinking about the fucked-up scene I had just encountered, and how weird Terry had been with me, how aggressive she had behaved with me.

Then, like a lightbulb came on, it all started to make sense. Why Terry had been so nice at school, but weird at home with Shell in their apartment later that same night. Why she had been acting so off last night, and again at the Plaza Hotel while on her phone, whispering. Why we'd heard her tell some other woman she loved her.

It was all clear to me now. "Dummy," I thought. Terry was up to no good. It was not my business, but I liked Shell. She was nice, so sweet and kind, and truly didn't deserve to be deceived in this way.

I met Carole and Smokey outside the house, still smoking and waiting of me.

"Did you take a shit out there?" Smokey asked. "You were gone forever, bud." She and Carole laughed, and I did, too.

"Naw. Just finding the perfect spot for my precious piss."

We all laughed some more. Then we went back inside and rejoined the party. Carole and I sat on the floor and started playing caps. Smokey was laughing, and all the women were so cool.

Just then, the phone rang.

"Terry?" someone yelled. "It's Shell."

My eyes got big. I knew what I had just seen out back moments ago. I knew Terry wasn't inside. And now Shell was on the freaking phone looking for her.

"She's outside," I yelled.

"Hey, sweetheart," I heard the woman who'd picked up say.

"She's outside smoking a butt. We'll have her call you when she gets in, okay?"

I don't know if that ever happened.

It was just Carole and I in the hallway, playing caps. I decided to share with her what I had witnessed outside with Terry. Carole was stunned, and also immediately pissed off. It seemed everyone loved Shell. I guess Carole was closer friends with Shell than I had realized. And maybe, at that moment, I was pissed off at myself for telling her. If I'd realized they were that close, I probably wouldn't have. I was getting to know this group quickly.

Carole got up, furious. The game was over. Carole was over talking to Silver and a couple of others about what I had told her. Then she ran outside. Smokey and I followed her. Carole stomped all the way through the backyard and around the garage. They were still there, still making out, still hiding.

"Carole bounded around the corner and yelled, "Caught ya!"

Terry jumped, and so did the woman she was with. Carole started arguing with Terry. They were screaming at each other. All hell broke loose.

"What the fuck are you doing?" Carole shrieked.

"You know we've been done for a while now," Terry yelled.

"Then just tell her and break up with her," Carole continued.

"Don't put her through this. This is just mean and fucked."

They were heatedly discussing the situation when Terry looked over at me.

"Thanks a lot," she said. "You're a great friend eh?"

"Sure thing, pal," I replied.

I didn't know what else to say. I wasn't mad, but Terry sure was pissed at me for telling someone. Smokey was all up in my face, too, now. I hadn't had time to tell her what was going on, but she had figured it out.

I wasn't going to let Terry bully me, though. This wasn't my fault. I wasn't the one fooling around on my sweet, nice girlfriend. Terry turned me off, then, now that her true colours had shown. Or maybe they had always been showing, but, because she was my first, real lesbian friend, I had ignored all the signs. But, had I? I noticed her weirdness, but it was as if I had been trying to convince myself there must be a better reason for it all.

Carole was still pissed about Sheri, the "other woman," who Carole and Smokey said they didn't really know. We found out later that she was new in Sudbury, also went to Cambrian, and was in the same course as Terry. Carole and Smokey had met her only once, a few months prior, at another party Terry had conveniently brought her to. Terry had introduced her to everyone there.

Terry and Sheri left. We watched them get into Terry's car and speed away. Carole stomped inside and grabbed the phone in the kitchen. Smokey and I were right on her tail, watching her from behind, wondering wide-eyed what the hell she was doing. It was suddenly all clear.

"Shell? It's Carole. I'm here at the party. No, no. Terry just left.

Sped away in her car after I caught her with that woman Sheri from school she's been hanging out with."

I could see Carole listening, but I couldn't hear Shell at all, because the women and music were still so loud at the party. I could only see Carole nodding. She was saying, "Yes, yes."

In that moment, I felt like I was shrinking. I felt absolutely shitty. Like, holy shit, Carole's on the phone telling Shell what happened. Is she that drunk?

I turned to look at Smokey.

"Smokey, she's on the phone with Shell!"

I was upset and she put her arm around me.

"Not your problem, bud," she said. She was right, but I felt responsible. I also didn't want the women to hate me. I had come into their circle of friends and started all this shit with my big mouth. It didn't turn out that way, though, thankfully.

We continued to watch Carole on the phone with Shell. she talked to her for quite a while. Her body language and facial expressions went up and down with her emotions and each sentence. She started to cry. Smokey and I leapt to our feet and went to her. We put our arms around her from both sides. She was completely sandwiched in our embrace, and we held her for the rest of the conversation.

When she finished the call with Shell, Carole went over to the fridge, grabbed a beer, and chugged it.

"Smoke a joint?" she asked me.

"Fuck, yeah, pal. You got it."

And the three of us went outside once again and smoked a joint. We talked it all through and hugged. Carole cried as she explained that she had seen Terry with this woman a few times and felt responsible for how long it had gone on without Shell knowing. She couldn't stand it anymore and couldn't help herself from telling Shell. But she felt bad, because now Shell had to deal with this all on her own.

We tried to console Carole. I told her how brave I thought she was, and how right she had been to tell Shell. Even though we were all drunk, it had been the right thing to do, because at least they'd have to deal with it now that the truth was out.

Smokey then cracked a joke and we all laughed. The three of us sat down on the steps leading from the house and drank and talked for what felt like hours, as lesbians came and went. Smokey had successfully moved our conversation away from Terry and Shell, and we were back to telling jokes and feeling less stressed from it all.

When we went back inside, the women had put their guitars away and the party had dwindled down to a few girls all just hanging about chatting in the barely lit living room.

"I guess that's our cue to go, bud?" Smokey said to me.

I agreed and so did Carole. I decided I was fine to drive. But, of course, I was not.

In Sudbury in the nineties, everyone drove after drinking. It was what we did. There weren't taxis in Sudbury back then. Or they may have had one car, maybe. But, it wasn't something anyone ever did or could afford to do. As long as you could see straight, you were good enough to drive; that's how we all grew up. That was what we'd seen our parents do, and that's what we did. We honestly didn't think anything of it; it was entirely normalized. Now, when I think about it, I'm shocked, but it was the way it was then.

I drove Carole home and as she got out of the back of my car when we dropped her at her place. She came around and hugged me through my open window. Then she ran around to Smokey's side and hugged her through her open window, too. We were all gushing with each other, talking about seeing each other at practice next Thursday, and how we couldn't wait. As I was backing out of her driveway, I yelled over to her.

"You're so damn righteous, girl. I'm going to call you Miss Carole!"

"I love it," she yelled back. "And, I'm going to call *you* Miss Elaineous!"

4

———

TOUGH GIRLS

Monday, back at school, I was nervous to bump into Terry. I was feeling all kinds of shitty about what had transpired with all of us at the party. But, it wasn't my fault she had been fooling around on her girlfriend. I suppose I could have not told anyone, but I had done it because I felt extremely comfortable with Miss Carole. Also, I grew up with loyal parents who would never have thought of doing such a thing, even though they often hated each other. There was no use putting someone through all that pain, for no reason. People should just break it off. Life goes on.

I talked myself out of my anxiety. My classes that day were normal, until my Law professor started class by asking me to stay afterwards to speak with him. That worried me. I was trying hard to remember the last exam I had cheated on, or what I might have done wrong in his last class, but I couldn't recollect.

After the class with our very tired, totally worn out, retired CO from the Cecil Facer Youth Centre was over, I sat at my desk and waited until everyone had left to speak with him.

"Elaina, I have got some big news for you," he exclaimed.

"A colleague of mine at Windemere, a medium-security, male

youth facility in Val Caron, has reached out looking for strong women to join their force. I mentioned you to them, how confident you are, and how big and strong you are."

"Really?"

My eyes felt like they were bulging out of my head as I listened to every word he was saying. I was wondering if this was real.

"Yes. And I mentioned that you'd probably be interested in going for an interview for a possible position soon."

"But I haven't finished the course."

"They don't care about the degree. They need women now. It's been mandated by the province, and they need to hire women ASAP."

"Really? I'm um …."

"The facility manager is expecting your call. I highly recommended you. I think you would get this job if you wanted it, Elaina."

"Wow. I'm so thrilled. Thank you, Al."

That was his name. We all used first names with the teachers at Cambrian College.

"Can you call her today?"

He passed over a little card with her name and number on it.

"I promise I will call her on my lunch hour today, Al. Thanks again."

I left the class and ran to the lunchroom to tell all my classmates what Al had wanted with me. I was sure they would all be wondering. Sure enough, when they saw me coming, they all looked up from their euchre game.

"Hey, Woman. What's up? What did big Al want?"

Most of the girls in my course called me Woman. It was something one of the other girls had started, and it had caught on.

"He's lined me up for a job," I said. "I'm to call this woman today. It's for a job at the boys correctional facility out in Val Caron."

"Yeah, I've heard of it. Windemere, right?" one of the guys in my program said.

"Yeah, that's it." I was excited, and they could all tell.

"Congrats, Woman!"

"That's amazing. I'm so happy for you. When are you calling her?"

Their questions were all coming at me.

"I'm going to go call her now and then come back and let you all know how it goes, 'kay?"

"Great!"

I was walking out of the lunchroom to find a quiet place to make my call when I, unfortunately, walked right by Terry.

Damn. I had forgotten about Terry for a minute there.

"How's it going?" I asked. I wasn't going to not say anything, right?

"Terrible, Elaina. Thanks for asking."

"Hey, I'm sorry you got caught with your pants down."

"You didn't have to bring the girls back there. You didn't have to say anything. You could have just minded your own business."

Now she had my steam engine revved up, and there was no turning back.

"Yeah, well, don't invite me over to meet your beautiful and loving girlfriend if you aren't going to be a good lover to her."

"Elaina, I brought you over to meet her because I was going to hook you two up," she cried. "I knew she'd love you and I wanted to line her up with someone awesome that I knew she would be crazy about before I broke up with her. To soften the blow."

"You what?" I honestly could not believe what I was hearing.

I was still mad, and now also completely in shock. It was all making sense. Why she had been so busy doing this and that and not hanging with Shell and me on the night she'd invited me over to their place. Why it had been Shell and me sitting and talking all night long, while Terry was distracted, going in and out to do laundry.

"Holy fuck, you're messed up," I said.

I turned and walked away. I couldn't handle this conversation anymore. And, I had my call to make, which was way more important that being drawn into Terry's drama.

When I got into an open space on the main floor of the campus building, I found a common area I liked. It had open seats and tons of plants, and a couple of pay phones. I picked one, plopped my books down, and sat on the bench beside the phone. I reached to get the card that my prof had given me out of my back pocket. Then I stood up to toss a quarter into the phone and dialed the number.

"Hello? Windemere Correctional Facility. How may I help you?"

"Hello. This is Elaina Martin, and I'm calling to speak with Tanya Forstell. She's expecting me."

"One moment while I find her." The receptionist put the phone down. I could hear people talking. There was a lot of commotion on the other end. It sounded like a busy place.

"Hello, Elaina? This is Tanya, Windemere's facility director."

"Yes. Hi, Tanya. My Law Professor Al Bentley at Cambrian gave me your number and said you were looking for some smart, strong women?"

"Yes, we are, Elaina. Can you come in for an interview tomorrow?"

"Wow, that's fast."

"Yes, we need someone to start right away. Can you come in at two p.m. tomorrow to meet with me and the facility owner Barb Morse?"

"Absolutely I can. Yes."

"Do you have a pen? Can you take down the address? We're at 1440 Longstanding Road, in Val Caron. It's a big, four-storey house with a lot of cars in the driveway, and a big, white van that says Windemere on it."

"I'll find it and see you at two tomorrow. Thank you so much, Tanya."

"Sure thing, Elaina. I look forward to meeting you and adding you to our great team."

Adding me to her team? Holy shit. Her saying that got my heart racing. This was all happening fast.

As soon as I got off the phone, I decided that if I was going to this interview tomorrow I'd better get home tonight after school to my folks' place. I'd have to get a good sleep, figure out what I was going to wear, and get ready for my interview.

When I got back to the table in the lunchroom, the entire gang was still playing cards.

"I'm not coming out to the residence tonight, gang," I said to my friends. But, I was looking directly at Rachel. I knew she was the one who would be the most affected by that. She didn't let me down.

"Again?" Rachel blurted out. "We didn't see you last week, nor on the weekend, and now tonight? I don't like this at all." She looked down and pouted.

I went and sat beside her and gave her a hug. I promised her I'd come get her after my interview tomorrow and after class, take her home to the residence, and spend the night there with her. She beamed.

I couldn't focus on the rest of my classes. I was too excited and scared about tomorrow. I wanted to go home and get ready right away. I wanted to tell my dad. He would be so proud about this. So, I did.

I grabbed my packsack full of books and said goodbye to everyone. I left Cambrian, walked out to the parking lot, got in my car, and drove home to Coniston.

When I got there, I started searching for clothes that would make me look big and strong. I thought black. Yes. Black was a good, strong colour. I put my black pants on, the ones I wore to funerals, which seemed to happen every year in my family. I added my black sweater, black belt, and my brown leather jacket. "That'll look tough," I thought.

I called my sister Dott to tell her about the interview and spent an hour on the phone with her. She was feeding her new baby. Dott made me feel so much better about my nerves and the interview. She was my confidante, the first person I told I was gay, and the first person to love me just the same. My big sister; I loved her so much.

One after the other, I could hear my parents arriving home from work. First, my mom who arrived at about four-thirty, after her last school run. She drove a school bus. My dad would usually arrive home closer to five-thirty, after his long drive home to

Coniston from the Loeb warehouse in Sudbury. When I heard pots and dishes start to get moved around, I knew both my parents were settling into dinner and it was time to go up and tell them my news.

I started explaining about my Law prof, Al, asking me to stay late. I made the story all dramatic, and they were both watching me and into it. I told them everything. My dad was grinning and so proud. My mom was already on the phone, bragging to my cousin Joyce, who she hung out with almost every day. Joyce lived down the street from us. She was a busybody and my mom's best friend.

My parents were thrilled, and I was, too. I couldn't wait. I grabbed a plate of shepherd's pie and headed back down to my basement to eat dinner. After that, to try and calm myself, I strummed my guitar for a little bit and otherwise had a quiet night at home.

The next day, I got up bright and early, although my appointment for the interview wasn't until two p.m. I had asked Dott if I could go over to her place so she could give me some more interview pointers. She agreed and said she'd help me prepare. That made me feel a bit less nervous.

When I arrived, Dott had just put the baby down and was delighted to see me.

We sat in the living room. She drilled me with basic questions that I should have quick answers to, and we came up with the answers together: "What are your best attributes?" "What are your hobbies?" Why do you want a career in corrections?"

That last one stumped me. I had never wanted a career in corrections before starting at Cambrian. So we talked about it. Dott knew my situation. She knew everything. She knew that a guy at my dad's work had told him about the Corrections program at Cambrian and that they were looking for big, strong women to apply. Dott and I figured out the Corrections program at Cambrian had been looking for women to take the course, because the institutions were looking for women. That's why this opportunity came specifically to me. The main reason I got the interview was that I was a big and strong, woman. So, we focused on that for a little bit. In hindsight, thinking about how I inadvertently found myself in corrections, I can't help but think of the ways young folks are recruited into these systems.

Dott kept on me with questions: what did I do to keep in shape? Why was I so strong? After a while Dott made us lunch and we continued our chat. The baby woke up and Dott let me feed her from her little bottle. She was the smallest, sweetest little girl. She had been born premature and was tiny for the longest time. But she was special—our first baby in the immediate family.

We finished feeding the baby, then had lunch. Dott wanted to send me to my interview with a full belly, she said. That way, I'd be ready for all the questions. I believed her. I've always believed Dott.

It was one o'clock and it would take me at least thirty minutes to drive out to the facility in Val Caron. I hadn't been there before, so I wanted to leave and go find it. I wanted to be there early, ready and waiting. Dott kissed and hugged me, and wished me luck, and I was on my way.

It was a quick drive from my sister's place in New Sudbury to the Lasalle and Notre Dame intersection where I'd turn right and down the highway to Val Caron. I knew the area a bit. My brother John lived out there, and I had been to his house a few times to hang out.

I was thinking about all the questions Dott had asked me, while watching intently where I was going, so as not to get lost and waste any time. I found the road I was to head down. It was a long, country farm road. I was driving by farms and fields and then, all of a sudden, there it was. I saw the four-storey house. It was massive.

If I hadn't known it was a facility, I would have thought it was the house of a rich person who had lots of vehicles. There were no signs, no fences. I don't know what I had been expecting, but it wasn't how I'd thought it would be. It was, quite simply, a very big house, not like a jail or institution.

I pulled into the vast driveway and parked, trying not to block anyone in, since I didn't know how long I'd be there. I sat and watched the house. You couldn't see anything from outside. The blinds were all shut and, although there were lots of cars in the driveway, I couldn't see any people.

At ten minutes before two, I walked up to the door and rang the doorbell. A smiley woman answered the door.

"Hi, Miss Martin? Tanya is expecting you."

I was surprised. I hadn't thought it would be so formal, I guess.

The woman brought me through the house, which was empty. I was wondering where all the boys were. The outside of the building made it look like a house, but the inside was definitely an institution. Everything was numbered and locked, and every cupboard and door had a sign on it.

I followed as she rounded a giant kitchen with long tables that had benches to either side. It looked like those tables fed a lot of people. The woman led me around another, multilevel space with couches, then down some stairs to Tanya, who was sitting in her office, on the phone, when we arrived. She motioned for us to come in and pointed at a chair across from her for me to sit down in. She signalled to give her a second, that she'd be done soon. I sat, and the nice woman who had shown me in left us.

Tanya got off her call and greeted me. She was a spitfire of a woman; that was obvious right away. Even on the phone, she was tough and direct, and loud and confident. I liked her instantly.

Tanya spent the next fifty minutes speaking with me. It was a very informal interview compared to what Dott and I had practiced. We had a good chat, though, and I figured she got all the information she needed, because, finally, she looked at me and said, "Elaina, you've got the job if you want it!"

I was stunned. I was terrified. I was quiet. Then I felt like she was kind of rushing me out, saying she had another appointment. But she looked at me before either of us stood.

"We need to start training you this week," she said. "If you want the job?"

It was only Tuesday. I was in school. I didn't know what to say. I hadn't thought about this part. I'm not sure any of us had thought about what would happen if I got the job. We hadn't practiced me getting it. I was thrilled but scared out of my mind.

"Um, I. It's just …."

"Listen," she said.

"I realize you have things to figure out. You'd need to quit the course at Cambrian, because our shifts here are sixteen hours long, and you'd work three days on, then get three days off."

Tanya went on to describe the working conditions and shifts that the correctional officers all worked there, including overnights. I was amazed, absolutely thrilled about everything she was saying.

"I'll take the job. And I'll start when you want me to," I said.

She smiled and her voice got louder.

"Excellent, Elaina."

She got up and hugged me. That was surprising to me. This woman had been very serious up until that point. But now she was happy, I guess.

I later found out she'd had a target to reach and had been ordered to have women start at the facility right away. My confirming I would take the job meant she could call the ministry and tell them Windemere had done what was mandated.

Tanya looked at her own schedule, then went over to a giant staff schedule up on a large board.

"I would like you to train for twelve hours with Ed this coming Thursday," she said. "And do a twenty-four-hour shift from six a.m. to six a.m. Friday. Can you make that work?"

"Yes," I said firmly. "What should I wear? Will it be twelve hours straight?"

She explained more about the training shift, and that I'd be learning how to be a "one-on-one" guard, something they needed a woman for.

I now had a ton to do and I didn't quite know where to start. I started driving back to Coniston. I was thinking about my classmates, how I'd said I'd come over tonight and hang with them. But I had to now figure out all my shit, and definitely couldn't go to the res to hang out.

Going would mean partying hard, like we always did there, and I could not afford to be drunk or hungover this week. It was Tuesday and I would be starting my first training shift on Thursday. I had lots to do beforehand.

As I was driving, I thought about many things, and each thing had a level of stress attached to it that was instantly exhausting to me. Like, how would I quit school? What would my dad think, when he had paid for half of it? What about my classes, my profs? What about my grades? What about my parents and staying at their house? Would I get my own place again? What about the res and my friends and classmates? What about Rachel?

Then, I thought about being a correctional officer, head-hunted right out of college, and how I'd be making big money right away and I'd never have to see Terry again, and I started to smile.

5

THE RIGHT STUFF

I had my first training shift Thursday to Friday, and it knocked me right on my arse. I slept until three p.m. after getting home around seven in the morning.

I still felt shitty for standing Rachel up, and not having any time to spend with her and the gang. I had spoken with her on the phone and filled her in. She was happy for me, but also sad. I could hear it in her voice. I felt like I should connect with her and my other buds from Cambrian residence, but my instinct now was to call Smokey instead.

I had spoken to Smokey earlier in the week, as well, to tell her about my sudden life upheaval and let her know I couldn't make it to the game this Thursday with The Right Stuff, since I had to work. It was hectic trying to explain everything that had gone down, so I told her I'd catch her up more the next time we hung out.

The week flew by and I couldn't help but think of how chaotic everything was and how much my life was changing. It was all happening so fast, it was hard to catch my breath.

Towards the end of the week I called Smokey. I wanted to be with my new, gay friends. It's not that I didn't love my residence gang, but they were all straight, with the exception of two people who were in the closet. It wasn't that fun anymore. Or maybe I just wasn't looking forward to it anymore. My new fun was laughing all night with Smokey. That's what I wanted to do.

Smokey was working under a car out in her yard when I called. Tracey answered. She had the day off from work and we chatted. She mentioned they had been talking about me earlier that morning, and that Smokey had wondered if I'd be around this weekend.

"How's your new job, Elaina?" Tracey asked. "Congrats, eh?"

"Thanks. It's pretty over the top, actually. I can't believe it; it's all happening so fast. My first training shift was yesterday. And I have to quit school. I'm going to have to move out of my folks' place, and I have a ton of friends from class all pissed at me. I need a drink."

"We can fix that," she laughed. "Wanna come over? We're heading to a party at Linda's tonight and you're more than welcome to join us. I'm sure she wouldn't mind if we brought you along."

"I'd love that, Tracey. I need to let off some steam. What time should I come over?"

"Anytime, Elaina. Smokey will be so happy to see you. Maybe I'll surprise her and not tell her."

"Okay. I'll just grab a shower, get dressed, and head over. I'll be about an hour, probably."

"Great. We'll see you then."

"Thanks, Tracey."

She was so sweet to me, as sweet as Smokey was, but hell to the no not as funny. Smokey was sweet, but also hilarious.

I couldn't stop thinking about my training shift the day before, and everything that had happened in just one shift. It was all swirling in my mind. I went over the details of my day at the facility while I got myself out the door and on my way to Smokey's place.

I was thinking about Ed, my boss and the person who was training me. When my shift was over this morning, he told me that I was a natural. He was a nice, down-to-earth guy. He was extremely good-looking, and probably in his forties, or older. He was single, but another staff member mentioned to me that he used to date the owner of the facility, so that was interesting. It likely meant he was still closely connected to the management. Good to know, I thought.

Ed showed me an enormous amount in one day. There were a lot of procedures to follow on the job, and I needed to take notes in a logbook about every single thing that went on during my shift. I was told I would have to do that for every shift I ever worked, writing down everything that happened. Incident reports were a different thing and took a bit longer to fill out.

"Try not to let shit happen, so you don't have to fill out paper-work," he said.

Before I was finished my shift, Ed asked me how I felt. He had given me a few tasks so he could check me out during my training shift. I could tell almost each time that he was testing me.

One of the things Ed asked me to do was manage a one-hour one-on-one session with one of the inmates. It was a boy who was on suicide watch and in solitary confinement because he was self-destructive. My job was to sit in the room and make sure the kid didn't hurt or kill himself. I thought, it's a padded room, right? What can he do? I had seen the room earlier when I had received a tour of the place. I had never seen anything like it and it piqued my curiosity, and now, right away, I was getting plunked into it.

I accepted the challenge with a calm, no-problem attitude, which seemed to please Ed. I was acting calm on the outside, but I was terrified on the inside.

Ed explained some of the boy's history, and that they were working on regulating his meds. But, for now, he was all over the place, and he had been suicidal for days.

Ed brought me into the room and told the male staff member who was in there that he could go on break.

"Carl," Ed said to the kid, "this is Officer Martin, who'll be with you for the next hour."

The kid looked up from where he was sitting on the floor. His knees were up under his chin, and his arms were wrapped around them. When he saw me, I smiled at him, and he looked down again. I took a seat where I had seen the other officer sitting. Then Ed walked out. It all seemed easy enough.

About five minutes after Ed had left, he heard screaming and rushed back in. He could immediately see I had the kid in a fully restrained position.

You see, when I first got into the room, the kid was completely quiet, just sitting calmly, facing down and not towards me. I figured this would be easy, this quiet kid. Piece of cake.

When the kid, Carl, heard the door close and lock behind Ed, he very slowly turned around to look at me. I smiled at him again. I noticed he had red, bloodshot eyes and a wild grin on his face. He made this face at me that seriously scared me. I was startled.

Then, just like that, he sprung up on his knees and started hammering his head against my chair, the chair I was sitting on. I could feel him smashing against my leg at the same time. It was violent. He was smashing his head, over and over, and as I jumped up, he grabbed the entire chair, dove right for it, and continued to smash his head against it.

I realized oh, damn, this is why I'm in here.

For just that second, I had been shocked, but I snapped out of it. I grabbed his arms and pulled him back off the chair and overtop of me. He was now fully on top of me, with his back to me, as I maneuvered to restrain him. It was hard, and, for a second, I might have worried whether I could do this, but I had to. This kid had already done some damage; I could see his eye blowing up. So I did what I had been taught to do and I took care of it.

Carl was a fourteen-year-old boy, and despite his young age, he was almost six feet tall and nearing two hundred pounds. He was also tremendously emotional and had started screaming his head off the second I touched him to put him into that hold. He kept yelling that he was going to kill me and then himself. That did scare me, but what it also did was ensure I wasn't going to let this kid go. What, to kill me? Forget it. I held on for dear life.

That was when Ed threw the door open and found me wrapped around this kid in a full lock. He called for some of the others to come and see, and they stood smiling and nodding. I was watching them while trying to maintain my hold.

"She'll be great," I heard one of them say.

"You okay?" Ed asked me.

"Yes?" I was trying to act as cool as a cucumber.

Ed was an old-school correctional officer, the kind who would do things like throw kids through walls. The officers and Ed chuckled and he directed them to get in and assist me. They did, and Carl calmed, eventually. Meanwhile, I was shaking, since I'd had to keep up steady force to hold the kid in that position. My nerves were shot.

When I was done in that room with Carl, Ed had me hang out with the other boys to get acquainted with them all, and to get a real feel for the place. The majority of the boys were all sitting in this giant, multilevel room that was used as a living room space. It had a huge fireplace that was never used, but that looked gorgeous. The TV was the only thing in the room that the boys were interested in, so all eyes were on that. It gave me a good opportunity to check them all out.

I stood there in the doorway watching them all watching the TV. There were taller, older boys, just under the eighteen-year cut-off, spanning down to the smallest fella, who was only ten. He shouldn't have been there, but his brother was at Windemere, and with no parents, they put him in, too.

They all just looked like average teenagers, just chilling, watching TV. I would come to learn that evenings, after they were in their rooms for the night, was when the worst shit always went down.

At the end of my shift, Ed told me I had done a great job. He was very impressed and asked me how I liked it. I said I loved it. I liked the place and the layout, and I liked the other officers I had met. Most of the boys were okay, too. I said I couldn't wait to come back for another training shift.

"Another training-shift? You only get one of those, kiddo," Ed laughed.

"I'd like to start you as soon as possible as full-time, frontline staff," he said. "You can work as my second for the first month, and I'll teach you everything I know. I like you. I think we'll work well together."

His confidence in me was rewarding and made me feel awesome. He was a big boss at the facility, and I was surprised he wanted to make me his partner on shifts. I would later learn that he had been told he would have to have a woman working with him, because of some complaints that had been lodged. I don't know what happened, but other staff told me some stuff one day in the staff quarters about Ed having been written up because some of the boys had said he was too rough with them. I didn't care about Ed's past. I was just pleased that he wanted to work with me.

"When will I start, Ed?" I asked.

"Let's see," he said.

He walked over to the large staff schedule on the wall and looked it over.

"I'm just finishing my three days today, and now I'll be off until Monday at one. So that's when you'll come in, Monday at one. Actually, get here for twelve forty-five and prep for your shift. And bring a bag of clothes with you, because you'll stay here with me in the staff quarters until Thursday. We'll work one p.m. to one a.m. day one, then we'll work seven a.m. to one a.m. for the next two days. Then we're done for three days. Three on, three off."

He explained this all to me as I listened intently.

So, that was my first training shift. I felt great when I was done, but totally sore and tired. Then I had a full forty-five-minute drive back to Coniston afterward. That was way too long a drive for how I felt. I told myself that, if I stayed in this job, I'd have to move closer to the facility.

Now I was off until Monday afternoon, and it was only Friday. I knew I had lots to deal with, including having to drop out of school. I had only been in for just over a year of the two-year program. We had started our second year in September. Now it was November and I would be leaving. But, I knew it was the right thing for me to do. I was convinced it was my destiny. Having this job come to me like it had, I felt like everything was finally falling into place. That included having come out, finally finding and being comfortable with my true gay self; and meeting and having new, gay friends and a community of lesbians to hang out with, people who were just like me.

I had shit to do, a lot of it, and I should have been doing it today, since I had to go back to work on Monday. But I was tired and didn't feel like it. It would all have to wait. I couldn't wait to tell Smokey and Tracey and Miss Carole about my big week and everything that was happening, and, of course, to have another adventure with my new buddies.

6

___

WINTER SHENANIGANS

I partied with Smokey and Tracey, Miss Carole, and my new gang of Dykes all winter. House party after house party, we never stopped. Every weekend there seemed to be another party at another lesbian's place.

That was what we did in the early nineties. There really weren't any gay bars yet in Sudbury, so we gathered in houses and collectively made community and created entertainment for ourselves.

I kept working all winter long, shift after shift, three on, three off. In between, I would attend as many house parties as I could. My days off didn't always fall on weekends, so it was a crap shoot which parties I'd be able to attend.

I grew much closer to Miss Carole. She had broken up with her girlfriend and was single now, which made things extra fun. She was training up on the train tracks near Coniston for her job with CN, and she would pop into my parents' place to visit me. After she had stopped by a few times, they didn't even call me upstairs anymore; they just sent her down to my room. Half the time, she'd crawl into bed with me to wake me up.

I also started hanging out with two other Dykes, Tina and Brandi, whom I'd met through Smokey. They were OPP officers and we loved to meet up at parties. They always looked ecstatic to see me. I think it was because we were kind of in the same industry, or it felt like we were doing something similar, at least, so they had someone they felt they could talk shop with.

They had a big house up on Moonlight Avenue, and we'd sometimes party at their place. I enjoyed going there, because they had a big, black lab named Max. It reminded me of the black lab my dad had when he was younger. It got killed by a transport truck on the highway near our house in West Arm when I was a kid. I was too young to remember, but I remembered hearing all about it, and how much my dad had adored that lab. Also, and more importantly from my perspective, it was the reason we were never allowed a dog when I was growing up.

The parties at the cops' place were always great. They had a pool table in their basement, and the Dykes would play all night and party. It was where I learned to really play pool. Smokey and Miss Carole both taught me by taking turns partnering with me and teaching me as we went along. They proved that they were patient and loving friends, because I wasn't very good at first.

Too hard.

Too soft.

Scratch.

Miss Carole was adamant about teaching me to think three shots ahead, and she started training me like that right away. She would get down and eye the balls from table level. She'd point and say "Look, if you hit your ball just there," and she'd put her finger on the ball I was to hit, "and hold your cue just like this," and she'd put her finger on the end of the cue, "it will hit the ball you want and come back to you, so you can hit the next ball you want."

There are all kinds of lessons that still come back to me and, when

I see a pool table, I always jump to play at it, remembering them. I enjoyed the game. I was nowhere near as good as many of the other Dykes, mostly because they played in leagues, but it was fun.

It was March 1, 1991, and I had been working at Windemere since November. Things were going wonderfully, and it was time to move out of my folks' place, again. I had originally moved out of our family home when I was sixteen, right after graduating high school, when my mom and I got in our last big fight with each other.

I had moved back in with them after my Dad set me up to go to Cambrian College. He had asked me to come live in the basement, where I'd have my own space until I finished school. Now that I had dropped out of Cambrian and was making good money at the boys facility, it was time to go. I had hardly been at my parents' place over the past year and a bit. While going to college, I'd stayed at the residence with my friends almost every night until I ultimately came out as queer.

I got myself a small basement apartment off Lasalle Boulevard, on Apollo Terrace. The street was kind of in a shitty area, but I was familiar with it, since it was right across from the Montrose Mall. That's where the driver's licence bureau was, where I had taken driving lessons, and where I got my licence when I was sixteen. It was also not far from my sister Dott's sizable house in New Sudbury, and just a hop, skip, and jump to the main drag, which would bring me to work each shift. I liked it. The apartment was small, but it was mine.

The first night being there on my own was glorious. I felt so good being alone again and having only me there, who I could trust one hundred percent. Don't get me wrong. I trusted my dad, always; just not my mother. Living with her, I always had dreams she would come downstairs and kill me in my sleep.

I wasn't in my new apartment very much, either. Since I always slept at Windemere during my three on, three off shifts, I only slept at home half the time. I don't even remember now what that apartment looked like, probably because it was furnished and why would I remember someone else's furniture?

It was in the basement of a triplex and had its own entrance at the back of the house, which I liked, and a parking space. That was all I needed. I certainly wouldn't be having any parties there, but I could at least feel okay about bringing someone home with me.

My dad came over to visit me a couple of times to see my place and make sure I had everything I needed. He always seemed proud of my place, commenting on every detail, even if it wasn't mine. I always made sure I had a beer in my fridge for my dad's visits. He liked that; I think it made him feel special. He came by a lot in the year I lived there. When he and my mom ended up selling their house in Coniston only a few years later, they moved into a nice apartment complex just a wee bit up from where I had been on Lasalle, right beside the Lasalle graveyard. I'll admit that part always freaked me out.

It was now a quick in and out to work, though. It only took me twenty minutes, on a good day, to get to my facility. That was much better than the forty-five-plus minutes it could sometimes take me to get home to Coniston. And after a three-day shift at the facility, I was pooped. This all worked out great.

7

FIRST TIMER

I had heard about R Place, Sudbury's first gay bar, from Donny, one of the other correctional officers at Windemere.

Donny was very cool and had a gay twin brother named Danny. Yes, that's right: Donny and Danny. Donny was proud of his twin and excited to always talk about him with me. It shocked me to hear Donny speak so openly about his brother. But it pleased me, too, of course. Donny was beautiful, so I imagined Danny was similarly attractive.

Each shift we shared, Donny was keen to tell me stories his twin had shared with him about his gay-ventures. I had told Donny I was gay the first shift we worked together. I felt I just had to, at least with him. He was immediately cool with it, and boasted more often about Danny than I think he would have otherwise. I think I was someone who Donny could openly speak to about his gay brother. He just couldn't do so with the rest of his world. Or his family. It was still their secret.

That didn't surprise me at all. I wouldn't have wanted to be a gay guy in Sudbury at that time. It was so homophobic. The devastating effect of the AIDS pandemic had further enflamed what were already violently homophobic mainstream attitudes. Gay men were attacked and targeted all the time, especially in these smaller cities. I remember that people at the time believed that AIDS was strictly a gay man's disease. Society treated gay men like vermin. So, yeah, at home and with almost everyone else, it was a secret that Donny's twin was gay.

It felt good to be Donny's confidant, and I know he appreciated it, too. So, Donny and I became very close on the job. I'll admit, I thought he was also gay, but I never mentioned it. Years later, I found out he eventually did come out as gay as well, and that made me happy.

At the time, though, Donny was into weightlifting, and always acted heavily butch, a muscle man who liked fast cars and women. It was a good cover, and one I've since seen many a hidden gay man perform. I had this little gaydar going off inside me, though, when I met him, and it never went away.

When Donny told me his twin was going to the new gay bar in Sudbury, my eyes instantly widened, my face got hot and I jumped to my feet full of excitement, like I had just won something. A gay bar in Sudbury? I had never heard of such a thing. But I was immediately very interested.

"What gay bar? Where is it?" I certainly beamed with excitement as I pressed him about it. It must have been very new, because none of the lesbians I hung out with had heard about it yet. They certainly had never mentioned it, and I damn well knew they would have if they'd known about it.

It seemed like Donny was as excited to tell me about it as I was to hear it, which I loved. He explained that R Place was at the corner of Lasalle Boulevard and Notre Dame Avenue. That was in New Sudbury, at a major intersection I drove by to get to work every day. Donny said it was on the main floor of an office building, at the front, with a big parking lot, right along Lasalle Boulevard. It had a big, blacked-out window at its front. He said I couldn't miss it, that there were no signs on the bar or door or window, but that "R Place" was listed on the big, roadside sign pole that advertised all the businesses in that building.

Donny was adamant about how much Danny loved it there. He loved it so much, in fact, that he was now dating the bartender. Donny made sure to mention that he'd never actually been there himself. But, he had driven by and looked it over after Danny had gone on and on about it.

I smiled. I was delighted. I was sick of hanging out at straight bars.

It had been getting harder and harder to hang out in straight places now that I was officially out as a Dyke. I don't know if it was the way I wore my hair, or my confident stance, or my party-hard, attract-all-the-cool-people-to-me ways, but men in straight bars tended to hate me, and were always picking fights with me now. I knew it was because I was gay, since I was regularly being called a "fucking Dyke." Also, Sudbury is a relatively small city and, let's face it, everyone knows everyone. News of anyone being one of the only out gay people in the city got out fast.

I had grown used to it, I'd had to, but I hated it. It was hard on me physically, emotionally and psychologically. I was always preparing for a fight, because it was always happening. I'd be talking to a friend and some guy would come over and literally pick a fight with me.

For instance, one time, I was out with a couple of friends I had gone to college with. We were at Norma Jean's, a bar in the big Ambassador Hotel complex in Sudbury, on Barrydowne Road. A popular discotheque, it was a place where many of our friends from high school worked. I had been going there for years. That night, we were all having a good time. I was leaning in talking to a good friend of mine, like you do when you need to hear someone, but the music is too loud, so you gotta get in real close to talk.

Well, if you're a Dyke and you do something like that in a small, homophobic town, people assume there is something sexual going on. Then it's instant hatred and aggression. *How dare* I be leaning in, obviously doing something sexual in public?

That hadn't been what was happening; we had just been chatting. Nevertheless, some guy came over. I didn't see it coming. I never did. I was drunk and partying with my friends.

But this straight man came over, and he yelled loudly into my exposed ear: "Fucking Dyke!" I'm sure it was as loud as he could make himself. My entire body jolted, and I was pushed over by the force of it. He had scared the shit out of me, but mostly I was shocked. I had been getting used to straight men attacking me, but I hadn't been expecting him just then.

When I stood up pretty fast, he came at me again. He pushed me real hard in my chest. I was shoved back, and I hit the floor on my ass. My friends all came running at that point and jumped in. And I was rushed out of the place. Instead of everyone fighting for me and taking this guy to town, I was removed, like I had been the problem.

That guy, and the many other guys who did things like that, and worse, got away with it. They always did. I was the problem. And although my friends loved me, they must have, deep down, also thought that I was the problem. That hurt me. It was one of the reasons why, when I found my people, my gay people, my life changed so much for the better.

I was an outwardly butch, confident gay woman. Once I was out, I was out. I had spent enough years not knowing what I was. Now that I was sure, I was openly out to everyone.

My world had instantly, like overnight, changed for me, and it had turned into this extremely dangerous place for me. It had never been dangerous before. This was all new to me. I was gay now, and everyone knew it. I had come out while I was at Cambrian. Word got around fast and, quickly, men didn't look at me the same way anymore; they all looked at me like they were angry.

It was instant how I had gone, in every space, from being thought of as this party person to being "the Dyke." I didn't change the way I walked, or looked, or groomed my hair, but now, this public knowledge of my sexuality translated into this violent public policing.

I was feeling hatred just for being me, now, and it was no longer safe for me to hang out at any of the bars in Sudbury. All the bars were straight, and at every bar I knew at least someone, so the same things would keep happening, no matter where I tried to hang out.

Finding R Place was a dramatic and transformative awakening. And it couldn't have come at a better time. Learning about this new bar, I couldn't contain my excitement. I planned to stop in on my way home after my stint at the correctional facility. I was almost done the three-day shift Donny and I were both on.

I was tired and wanted to get home. My routine after a three on, three off shift at Windemere was usually the same. I would sleep a lot. Honestly, I mostly just slept on my days off. I was always exhausted, between the boys at the facility, all of their issues, the case reports, and generally being inside the institution. The hard work of dealing with humans who have been shunned from society is hard on the heart, mostly.

Also, although we had beds at work, in our staff area in the basement of the facility, I never slept well—or at all—down there. We were supposed to sleep two nights, from midnight until six a.m. Meanwhile, overnight staff came in and ensured all the boys were in their rooms for those six hours and that "the place didn't burn down" while we took a break to catch some Z's.

There were good reasons for not getting much sleep while at the facility. For one, down in our staff room, the other staff would drink heavily after their shifts, playing euchre, ordering in food, laughing and/or crying, and talking. They perpetually talked about all the troubled kids we were dealing with upstairs, and the shit they'd gotten up to that day. The staff area was kind of like a little apartment for the COs. Though occasionally I would also drink and party with them, on the nights that I did want to sleep it was pointless to try, with all the agitated conversations happening around me.

So despite my fatigue at the end of my three day shift, I was bubbling with excitement about R Place, and decided I would have to stop there even before I went home and crashed out.

I mean, it was on the way home, and I had been thinking about it for three full days by then. I innocently asked Donny if he'd like to come with me, for a drink after work. We often did that. This time, however, his face screwed up and he got instantly defensive and cagey at the thought of being invited to a gay bar.

"Hey, slow down, bud," I said. "You were just all up in my face about the place, so I didn't think twice about asking you to come with me for a drink, like we do."

But Donny wasn't having it. It was a *gay bar*, he reminded me sternly, and he was *not gay*; his brother Danny was. Donny got so emotional not accepting my invitation.

"Fine, fine. No problem, buddy," I said in the end. "I'm gonna go check it out, though. Thanks so much for telling me about it."

No big deal. I was more eager than nervous, really. After gathering my shit after work and cleaning out my area downstairs in the staff room, I said my goodbyes to all the boys and the new shift staff, and I was on my way.

8

GOT ME FROM BEHIND

I drove down the big highway that takes you from Val Caron, where the facility was, into downtown Sudbury. R Place was at the intersection marking where you arrive back in the city. I put on my blinker, turned left and drove into the parking lot entrance, off Lasalle.

I drove right up to the big, blacked-out window that Donny had mentioned. I sat in my car for a couple of seconds, fixed my hair in the mirror, then hopped out. I looked back and up, and saw the big road sign with "R Place" on it. I smiled and turned to make my way to the door.

It was only five p.m. on a Thursday and I wasn't sure the place would be open yet. But right as I approached, what I eagerly assumed was an older gay dude came out the door, so I knew it was, and I walked past him and into the bar.

It was nearly empty. There were two guys leaned over at the bar, and two guys at a booth in the corner, but that was it. A big, burly, bearded fella at the bar saw me come in and look around.

"Welcome," he said.

I walked up to him at the bar.

"Hi," I said. "I'm Elaina. I was told this is a ...." I wasn't sure for just a second. I'd never been in an actual "gay" establishment before in my life. This bartender looked like a biker, so I was confused.

"You sure are new here, darling," he said. "Welcome to R Place, Sudbury's new gay bar. My name is Pete."

His eyes sparkled and his smile was genuine. And as I watched his lips mouth the words, I burst inside like my heart had blown up three times its size.

"Hi there. I'm so excited to be here."

"It's a bit quiet just yet, darlin', as people are still getting off work. But if you stick around, you'll see the place will fill right up."

I was coming apart at my own seams.

"Can I get a Canadian, please?"

"Now you're talking, sweetie." As Pete opened a bottle of Canadian and passed it over to me, he smiled at the guy sitting next to me who had seemed interested in my arrival and now turned to me in excitement,

"Elaina?" he said. "Like, Elaina Martin, the CO?"

I turned to see him, and it looked like Donny. But no, of course, it was Danny. He had heard about me from his brother. We squealed at each other like we had known each other for years, and hugged and danced around. We were ecstatic to finally meet.

I propped myself up at the bar by Danny and his boyfriend, who was the bartender, Pete, of course, and the party was on. I felt like I had died and gone to heaven hanging out with these two guys, in a new gay bar in Sudbury. I couldn't believe what was happening.

They were fun and exciting and gay, gay, gay. I had finally found my place, and it was R Place. As I sat at the bar laughing with Danny and Pete for hours, drinking and having a great time, more guys kept pouring into the place. I hadn't really noticed, because I was having so much fun with my new best friends. Then, just like that, the place was packed.

It was a Thursday night and almost nine o'clock now. The lights had been lowered, and I was drunk and happy hanging with Danny and Pete at the bar. I laughed and learned so much talking to those guys.

At some point, I pulled my stool back, hopped off, raised my arms to the ceiling, and yelled, "I'm home!"

Oh my goodness, the gay boys all laughed at me.

"Hurray for the Dyke!" one guy yelled out and we all laughed. I almost cried, I was laughing so hard and was so full of joy.

Pete was also R Place's manager. He and Danny told me about events they were planning to hold at the bar, and plans they were making for the future. It was all so exhilarating to me. The owner had opened the place as a restaurant originally, and they'd served food at the start. He'd had a Dyke cooking in the kitchen, but supposedly the Dyke cook and the owner got into a big fight and he kicked her out and closed the kitchen down.

Fridays and Saturdays were for dancing, but Pete and Danny said they wanted to do other things for Sundays. That was when I piped in.

"Hey, guys? You know, I play music and I know a few other Dykes who also play. We could come perform here and do a show sometime on a Sunday."

"That's amazing. We'd love that," said Pete. He was into it and we made a plan that I would come back another time, bring my guitar and play a few songs for him.

I had been hanging out with various Dykes since coming out, meeting every lesbian in the city one house party after another. I had started jamming with a bunch of Dykes who all played guitar and sang. We'd have lesbian house parties and the girls would all be playing Indigo Girls and Melissa Etheridge covers. I had largely been loving my new gay life.

Almost everyone at that time had the same experience as me. Once we were out and openly gay, there were no safe spaces for us in straight bars in Sudbury anymore. Either the men wanted to hurt us, or the women wanted to fuck you and then the men wanted to hurt us even more. It had been a tiring dance, and I was very relieved to stop jigging.

I'll admit I hadn't met a lot of gay boys in the first year and a half I was out. It was mostly women I had met. Being a Dyke, those were the parties I had been going to and, although there had been the odd gay guy hanging with us sometimes, they had mostly been all women.

After I told them about all the house parties and gatherings the women had been doing on their own, Danny and Pete were fully into the ideas I was coming up with for bringing Dykes into the place. They wanted to move those parties to R Place, and I did, too, eventually.

It was now one a.m. I was so tired, I was starting to slur my words. I knew that, although I had just had the night of my life, it was time to go home.

"Hey, boys. It's time for this Dyke to put her head down," I said.

"You seriously must be so tired girl," Danny said. "I know the hard job you have."

"Aww, thanks, Danny."

I hugged him hard. Pete jumped over the bar and gave me the

biggest hug. I kept thanking them both, telling them how this had been the best night, and how I'd finally felt like I was home.

It was true that I felt transformed in that space, as if, in one night, my life had developed deeper meaning, purpose, and a destination. I was euphoric.

"Bye! Bye!" I yelled over the music to everyone as I walked out the door and into the dark night of the parking lot. The lot was empty other than a couple of cars. The sky was black and the night's warm air was soft on my face. I was so pleased.

It was a beautiful night, and I felt such warmth inside me, like I had accomplished something incredible. I hadn't accomplished anything, in reality, other than finding my new bar. But, it was a space where I could be fully me and say and do what I wanted without reprisal or someone hating on me or trying to hurt me. So, it was heaven.

I truly felt at peace and the big, open empty parking lot was a perfect visual finish to a night like this. It was me and the world, and I was going to take it on, finally.

I was driving a New Yorker Fifth Avenue at the time, a hand-me-down car my father had given me. It was parked in front of the door where I had left it. I jumped in and started her up. I put the sedan into reverse and hit the gas to back up so I could turn around to exit.

Bang! Smash!

My body was thrown forward, then back against my seat, hard.

"What the fuck," I yelled. I was scared and in shock.

I looked in the rearview mirror. There was a fucking car behind me, and I had hit it. I had been bolting out of there in reverse and hadn't seen anyone in the parking lot when I looked. There hadn't been anyone behind me. What the actual fuck?

I undid my seatbelt and threw my door open. I leaped out and stood, stretching because the jolt had hit me so hard that I was all crooked and sore. An older gay guy bounded out of his car, mad as hell that I had rammed into him.

"What the fuck, dude?" I said.

"Where did you come from?"

We argued for a couple of minutes, both of us in shock and upset. Honestly, his car was a mess. My car was fine, but his hood was completely folded in two, up higher than his windshield. I hadn't noticed the bar had emptied, but the last few people who were still there all ran out to see what was happening. They had heard the loud bang and smash of the collision, the glass breaking, and us arguing about it. It was quite the commotion.

Pete came out and immediately went over and calmed the other driver down. Danny had his arms around me, rubbing my back and consoling me. We finally brought the energy down to a civilized conversation. We worked out insurance information and decided not to call the cops. I was obviously at a bar and had been drinking all night. That's where Pete had come in handy. He had been running the bar and immediately knew this wasn't a good scene. He needed to make it go away.

Pete worked out some arrangement with the guy. Thankfully for me, he was a regular at R Place and Pete knew him well.

Pete found someone to tow the guy's car. My New Yorker was fine. We agreed to call each other the next day, on my day off, to work out the final details. I said I'd pay for the damages. I got in my car and drove home, crawled into bed, put my head down, and passed out hard.

When I woke up the next morning, my head was sore and I was bone-tired. At first, I thought it had all been a dream, going to R Place, meeting Danny and Pete, the fun and the bar, the plans we had made, all of it. It all circled in my mind. A giant smile spread across my face when I realized it hadn't been a dream. It was all real.

Then remembering the accident ripped me from my pleasant thoughts. It was time to get up and call my insurance company, and the dude I'd rammed into last night. At least it had happened at the tail end of what was otherwise one of the best nights ever. I literally couldn't wait to go back.

But, more importantly, I couldn't wait to tell Smokey, Miss Carole and the girls this weekend.

After waking up and shaking off my stiff neck from the car accident, I called the guy whose car I'd hit and spoke with him about insurance and such. He was much nicer today than he had been last night when I'd hit him. We kind of just let it go and were pleasant with each other.

We decided I'd give him five hundred bucks to buy a new hood for his car, call it even, and not call the insurance companies. I figured that was fair. He told me he had gotten an estimate for a new hood and getting the other damages fixed. It would be nearly twelve hundred dollars. That wasn't much for him. He was a professor at Laurentian University at the time. But it had been half my fault, so I offered to pay for half, and he said he'd take five hundred dollars. That was more than fair. My car hadn't suffered any damage and, being that the cops weren't called and I didn't get in any trouble, I was happy with how things went down.

9

R PLACE

It was Friday afternoon now and I had planned to go back to Tina and Brandi's place for another gathering tonight so I called Smokey to set up a plan. After I told Smokey all about R Place, my night there, and the accident, she offered to come get me. That felt good; I didn't want to have to worry about driving tonight. I just wanted to let loose.

Smokey was thrilled to hear about R Place and suggested that we go there after we were done playing pool with the girls. I was down for that plan, and very glad I lived only a couple of blocks from there, so I could crawl home if I had to.

When we arrived at Tina and Brandi's place, the regular gang was there, the usual roster of Dykes who hung out with us most nights. They all surrounded me as I told them about R Place and the details of my night there. They were all excited. It was like we were going to Wonderland or something, given how excited we all were about it.

I'm pretty sure we cut the night short to head there; we just couldn't wait. Tina and Brandi couldn't join us, but Miss Carole,

Smokey, Mags, and a bunch of us went. We piled into Smokey's van and headed to R Place.

We were all completely lit, singing in the van, still drinking and smoking dope, all the way to the bar. There were eight of us crammed into it, most of us sitting and falling all over each other on the floor in the back. Smokey's van only had the two seats in the front. The back was open space, because she was a delivery person and used her van for work.

When we got to the R Place parking lot, it was midnight on a Friday and I got to instantly see the place in a different light from the night before. The parking lot was full, so we actually had to park at the back of the building and walk around. That worked out well. The van was more discreet back there.

When we walked into the place it was jam-packed with men. Some of them looked toward the door and smiled at us; others rolled their eyes as we stampeded into the place like a herd of cattle. The Dyke party was on like Donkey Kong.

I kept looking around at everyone. They were all so happy. The girls were so excited to be there. The music was loud, and the guys started coming over to meet us and intermingle, which made me happy. Danny came over as soon as he saw me, and I introduced him and his boyfriend, Pete, to all the girls.

"You really did bring us the girls, Elaina."

"I told you I would, brother."

We hit our bottles together and cheered. We ended up all staying there until four a.m. The bar had stopped serving at two, but we were all still hanging out in the parking lot and by the van behind the building.

Drunk lesbians and gay guys all over the place, sitting here, sitting there, talking, drinking out under the moon, and carrying on. It was a very special night, and it turned our lesbian lifestyle on its head. We did still have parties after that, and gatherings and get-togethers, for sure, but they mostly became for special occasions.

R Place became literally "our place," and we spent all spring hanging out there.

My new routine was: go to work, do my three on, three off, then go home, shower, change, and walk over to R Place. I didn't even need to call anyone to meet me there now. I knew all the regulars and would just go sit and talk to whoever was there, whenever I wanted. It was a community.

I loved it at R Place. It was a safe place in public, or, at least, it felt like it was in public. It was on one of the busiest, most popular streets in Sudbury, just discreetly subtle. It became the place where we could be openly gay and not worry about people trying to hurt us.

One of the best things about R Place was that the entire city of straight people, homophobes, troublemakers, and overall hateful people, didn't know it existed. Most of them didn't even think there was a "queer" community in Sudbury, and we didn't advertise it.

I think R Place may have run for its entirety without the straight community ever knowing about it. I don't remember any gay bashing ever happening there, or fights, or anything like that. Nothing like what I was about to experience in the coming years.

R Place was protected by the fact that no one around Sudbury would ever have thought there would have been such a place. We were under the radar, and that afforded us a certain safety.

Spring turned into summer and it was now routine for all the lesbians to meet and party at R Place. Pete got fired for something. I don't remember what. But he was let go, so Danny disappeared, as well, which made me sad.

A new guy took over managing. His name was Paddy. He was a

tall, good-looking, dark-haired cutie whom all the boys liked. He was nice, bilingual, and very serious about the job. He was also supportive of the lesbians, and into making plans with us for entertainment nights. We planned a reading night. We planned a craft night. Dykes on guitars became a regular Sunday afternoon event, and we now had regulars coming to hear us play music. It was all sweet.

I was still at Windemere and would go as often as I could, but I missed quite a few good times at R Place because of work. The girls were hanging out there every weekend now. I'd hear stories about the nights I missed, and I'd feel envious and resentful about having to work while my buddies were partying. I certainly made up for it on my days off, though.

R Place was fun, inside and outside. It was on the very most outskirts of Sudbury, literally at the crossroads at the end of the city, where if you keep going in any direction you soon end up in another community or town altogether. That helped with the privacy of the bar, and allowed people the freedom to hang out in the parking lot all night. We had parties in that lot, wild parties, with all of us outside, dancing and singing, under the big, lit-up sign that read "R Place." Hardly any cars would drive by us, it was so remote at that end of Sudbury at night.

One Friday, I planned to meet all the girls there, but it turned out no one was able to go. So, I was there by myself, which was fine. One of the gay guys I knew had propped himself beside me at the bar. He'd brought a friend with him and was trying hard all night to hook us up. I hadn't been with a woman yet. I had only come out months before, and was still feeling things out. I had kissed a couple of women and made out a bit with one woman, but that was it.

This woman was all over me, though, and it felt good. I got very drunk and we made out in the bathroom, then again in the parking lot. I didn't overly like her, though. I was just going through the motions. I thought I should at least get to see what fooling around with a woman was all about. She begged to come home with me when the bar was closing that night, but I made up some excuse to ensure that wouldn't happen. She gave me her number and asked me to call her, but I didn't. I hadn't given her mine, either, so I figured I was safe.

The next time I was in R Place was the following Thursday. After I got off work, I went for dinner with Smokey and Tracey. We were meeting Miss Carole and her new girlfriend at the bar. The second I got into the space, that same woman ran over to me.

"Did you lose my number?" she asked. "I was hoping to see you again."

I smiled at her and shrugged it off, laughing. Then I continued to hang out with my friends. I kind of ignored her. The slightest part of me felt shitty about it, but I just wasn't into her. She got the drift, I guess, because, from the corner of my eye, I noticed her leaving.

Paddy came over and told me that she had been at the bar almost every night, waiting for me to come by, since we'd made out last week. He said that each night they'd tried to reassure her that I usually stopped in at a certain time. They had wondered why she didn't have my number, and figured I probably hadn't given it to her on purpose. I wasn't ready for a relationship. And lesbians were intense, at least this one was, and it scared me.

Paddy's story made me feel even worse. I had only just met her and was still so inexperienced and apprehensive – no one had given me a roadmap to lesbian dating and her intensity overwhelmed my greenness.

10

SUDBURY WATER TOWER BATHHOUSE

Fall 1991 my best friend Benny moved back to Sudbury and I couldn't have been happier. Benny was my oldest friend, we grew up together and when Benny had left town, we were both closeted. Now he was home and we were both openly gay. "Life is so awesome," I thought. I couldn't wait to see Benny.

He'd gone to Carleton University in Ottawa for two years. I missed him and was thrilled when he reached out to my folks to tell them he was back. My dad called me at my apartment to say he'd heard from Benny, and to give me the new phone number he'd left so I could call him. This was big and wonderful news. I hadn't talked to Benny in a while. He had been six hours away in Ottawa, in school, and I had been working, and in school before that. Plus just life. We had largely lost touch for a couple of years.

I think we had seen each other briefly the previous Christmas. But, now he was home, and I couldn't have been happier. I called him up and made plans to go see him after my next shift, at his new apartment downtown.

Benny had gotten himself a small bachelor apartment. A few days later, I went over after work, and we smoked joints and laughed and got all caught up. We had lots to talk about, with all the coming out we had both done recently.

Benny talked about a boy he had loved in Ottawa, and I told him about my Corrections courses, and coming out while in school. Then I told him about R Place. We decided right then to go over for a drink.

When we arrived at R Place, Benny couldn't believe where it was located. We talked and laughed about how so many straight people would drive by every day and not even know what it was.

There was another new guy behind the bar. It was dead, because it was just after five. They only opened at five, so it was literally only Benny and me there, and the bartender. But, that didn't matter. We started drinking, and we partied with that bartender until others showed up.

When they did, they joined our party. We were in it to win it. Benny and I had always been a very lively duo. We just know each other so well, and it's fun to hang out and reconnect with someone like that after a long absence – particularly when you consider the excitement of sharing your queerness with each other for the first time. Add to that the fact that Benny is one of these socially infectious, outgoing and over-the-top funny people who naturally command attention, and you can imagine the excited energy our reunion provoked. We listened to Benny's animated stories, his gravelly voice, big eyes, and his hands waving all over the place. He had always been fun, but now that he was out as gay? He was unbridled.

I watched him putting on a show for our new friends. Sitting there, I thought back over the years, and all I could do was smile. Benny used to be the "good boy."

I mean, he's always been a good boy. He was class valedictorian of our high school, for Christ's sake, good grades, never in trouble, didn't smoke drugs, hardly drank. That was the Benny I'd grown up with. Now, he was out and loud and proud and fun, and a party animal, and I thought, wow, has he changed.

He stopped yakking for a second and looked at me.

"What the hell darlin'?" he said. "Cat got your tongue?"

"Nah. I'm just loving you hard, Benny. I'm enjoying how much you've changed over the years. You're a bad boy now, and I love it."

"That's your fault," he cried.

We all laughed. He would later tell me quite often that I was the one who'd smoked his first joint with him and had started drinking with him. I couldn't deny it though I'm sure university life and coming out in the big city of Ottawa had added some texture to his new ways.

I went to the washroom, and when I came out, Benny had the new bartender on his lap and they were making out.

"Hey, hey, rent a room!" I yelled at them. But I was smiling. Benny looked up at me, pausing the necking for a second.

"Get your own," he said.

We all laughed even more.

The place was packed now, and we were definitely the life of the party.

Benny and I had reconnected solidly, like we had never left each other's sides. It was beautiful, and it made me so happy to now share this part of our lives together. I couldn't think of anything that could be more perfect.

We partied at R Place until it was time to close up. Benny and the barman were definitely heading back to Benny's place. I had picked up, too, but I was going to drop Benny and this dude off at Benny's first.

The woman I'd hooked up with, MJ was super cute. In town for some Laurentian University event, she had been at R Place with a gay, male friend of her own. They'd both been hanging with us all night. I liked her and thought it was time I should have some fun.

MJ told me she and her work colleague were staying at the Ambassador Hotel while in Sudbury. I asked how they'd found R Place, when most of our own city didn't know it existed. She told me her brother, who was also gay, had been there the month before on a similar visit to the Big Nickel.

I decided to pack them all into my enormous car. Benny and his boy sat in the front with me on the long bench seat. MJ and her workmate were in the back. I drove up to Pine Street, where Benny's new place was. Once he and his man were out, MJ jumped in the front, and I gave my visitors to Sudbury a little tour.

We made our way back down Elm, and I showed them the downtown, which was pretty cool back then. We went up the big hill and I pointed out the water tower. My new friend was enthusiastic about how close and how big it was, and I immediately came up with a plan.

We continued up the Kingsway, while I pointed out places like the old Petro-Canada station I had worked at a few years before, and other landmarks. Then I saw the big lights and giant arch, and no, I don't mean McDonald's. I mean the pride of Sudbury, Deluxe Hamburgers, the original burger arch.

It was up ahead on the right. I could see the lights were still on. I revved the engine and drove up the hill into the parking lot. This was a place my high school friends and I would stop at, late, to pig out when we were drunk. Two of my high school friends had worked there, so we often got free food. It was a regular hang out.

Now it was a Sudbury landmark I was bringing my out-of-town guests to, and I bragged and told them all about it as we went inside. I ordered my favourite, chicken on a bun, with fries and sauce. It's all about the sauce, I kept telling them as they were trying to order.

"It really is something incredible. Wait 'til you try it."

The old man who owned the place, and who always saw me in there, yelled over.

"She's right. And she would know."

We all laughed. He knew I was the biggest fan of his food, and the sauce. We got our meals and sat at one of the iconic retro 50's diner-like tables. We giggled over our delicious Deluxe sauce as we looked out at the streetlights and the late-night traffic along the Kingsway.

When we were done, I drove them up the Kingsway, to the Ambassador Hotel, and pulled in. I was very familiar with the place, having partied with my straight friends at Norma Jean's a million times when I was younger.

The guy in the back seat jumped out right away. He told his friend he'd see her tomorrow, and he took off. I guessed he was giving us time on our own to make out. But, I had something else in mind.

I looked at her as she leaned towards me in the front seat, coming in for a kiss.

"Are you tired?" I asked.

"Hell no."

"Great," I said.

I pulled out of the parking lot and headed back up the Kingsway. She looked excited. She slid over my seat and snuggled up right next to me while I drove. My hand was on her lap, rubbing her leg, slowly making my way up her thigh.

I drove towards the downtown, but when I got to the Elm Street hill, instead of going straight back into the downtown core, I took this weird right turn. We went up this very steep hill on Fairview Avenue, up, up, up we went. She was holding on to me like we were on a rollercoaster ride. We drove to the top of the hill, then around a little bend, and into a parking lot.

"Get out of the car," I said mischievously.

She looked at me strangely, and, for a second, I think she got nervous. But then I smiled at her and she warmed up again. I got out of my side of the car, ran around to hers, opened her door, and pulled her out. When she stood up, she saw it above her. We were right under the giant Sudbury water tower she had been so excited to see when we drove by it earlier. I knew we could drive right up to it. My brother John had taken me up there once, to tell me how he had done acid and climbed the thing. He had been up there an entire night tripping on acid. I loved that story and relayed it to my new friend.

We laughed, and then we made out under the giant, baby-blue tower. We ended up sitting on the hood of my car, against the windshield snuggling and kissing until the sun came up.

It was a gorgeous night and I had a lovely time with her. When morning came, and the sun came up, we watched it and laughed at our full night of escapades. She mentioned she had a conference starting in a couple of hours, and that she should get back to shower and get ready. Someone was picking her and her friend up at eight to take them up to Laurentian.

So, I took her back to the Ambassador Hotel and dropped her off. I gave her a big kiss before she got out, and we exchanged numbers. I never heard from her or saw her again.

This would not be the last time I would take a woman up to the water tower. It became my spot, a spot I took all the women I would hook up with over the next few years in Sudbury. It was also a spot I would take friends, even if it was just to smoke a joint. It was so cool up there. But, I especially loved making out up there.

11

JUST BEFORE THE DAWN

Another work week of three on, three off shifts out of the way, there was some downtime for me ahead. I was always so fucking exhausted after my shifts at the boys facility.

It took a lot out of me, and I watched it take a lot out of all the staff there. It was not an easy job. It was dealing with lonely, forgotten youth, all suffering, in pain, and with mortality issues.

It was a sad place and it was starting to get to me. I was feeling low pretty often. I would feel low after a shift. Then, I'd get a few days off, recalibrate outside of the institution, and be able to snap out of it. Then, I'd go back to work and it would slowly creep into me again, this deep sadness.

I couldn't handle that part of the job. It was so sad to see all these great, sweet, and, in some cases very loving, lost, little humans all caged up together, being moved around by people who often didn't give two shits about them. It weighed heavily upon me.

And I started drinking a lot more on my days off. I would start almost immediately after my shift was over, and it wouldn't end until I went back to work. Then, we'd drink at night in the staff room, after the kids had gone to bed and the night shift had taken over. We'd kill a bottle of rye each night, usually. That was what Ed drank, and that's where I found my love of rye whiskey.

One thing my short time in corrections at Cambrian hadn't prepared me for was the immense psychological toll the job took on me. That's why the parties with all the Dykes made me so happy. For at least a little while, I could forget about the facility and all the sorrow there.

Miss Carole was going to be in a pool tournament this weekend, with her team. A few of us girls decided we would hop from bar to bar with her and cheer them on. It was Friday night.

We started at May's Tavern on Elgin Street, downtown. It was one of the roughest bars in the city, but was also full of old-school, hardcore Dykes on the regular. It was a place where anything and anyone could go and feel at home. No pretentions, no expectations, that was May's. It was run by ol' May herself and she was intimately connected to her neighborhood. She knew the local homeless, and fed most of them, too. She was an angel. Yet, she had ties to the bikers, and most "normal" folk in the city would never have stepped foot in the place. But I liked it, and it was full of lesbians, so it was awesome.

That night, it was full of Dykes playing pool. After the game was over, we jumped into our cars and headed over to the Plaza Hotel for the next round of games. We cheered all night as Miss Carole sunk each ball. I was likely the loudest; I usually was. I've always had a very loud voice that carries far. We were a rowdy bunch, all laughing and joking, as we usually did.

It was nearing midnight when we were done there. Miss Carole's team had won the day's rounds and would move up to the finals the next day. I offered to stuff everyone into my big car and take us down to R Place for last call.

"Hell yeah," they all screamed. "Let's go!"

The girls were yelling over each other and we were all yapping and talking and laughing while getting into my car. With the Fifth Avenue filled to the brim with Dykes, I headed over to R Place where we pulled into a full parking lot. It was just after midnight on a Friday night, after all.

When we got inside, we were a party heading into a party. To say the party inside got hell-raising hardcore just then would be an understatement. We rocked that little place, all dancing body to body. I'm sure the windows were shaking.

You gotta understand, this bar was not large by any stretch. I'd say around thirty feet long by twenty feet wide, at most. With us all dancing in there that night, we probably stuffed over fifty people into it. Not only were we body to body in the place, but we each had a beer in one hand and a cigarette in the other. It was the way it was back then.

We partied hard that night and didn't get out of there until nearly four a.m. That was another thing we would do often back then that you can't do anymore: stay late at the bar after it "closed." In other words, it didn't close. A bar would usually stay open as long as people were there spending money at it, drinking.

The next day was Saturday, and I just lay around my apartment and chilled out all day. I needed a day just to sleep and catch up on my energy.

I only had one thing I had to do this weekend, and that was have dinner at my sister Dott's place on Sunday. She was having family over for dinner.

My dad came by to pick me up. He wanted to have a few minutes with me before we got back to Dott's, where my mother would be, and my sister's husband, two people who got on both of our nerves. My dad seemed to be the only person who understood how negatively they both affected me, probably because they affected him similarly. Either way, he picked me up and we braced ourselves for a day with the family.

My brother John showed up, too. He was drinking, and that caused issues for my mother. The day was ruined by those two and their common dance around alcohol and shaming, and just the histrionics that went along with my mother. She loved embarrassing my brother, making him feel small.

I couldn't wait to get home. My dad took me back early, after dinner. He could see I was losing my patience with them all. My other sister Lena, with her crying ways, and her brooding husband were also painful. I had to get out of there. Dad saw all that in my eyes and took me home.

I didn't live far from Dott's place, only a five-minute drive, but Dad and I talked on the way. It always helped to get my dad's perspective on things, he was so patient.

"It'll all work out," he always said. "Try not to worry."

He always tried to focus on the positive. Honestly, living with my poisonous mother, I have never understood how he was able to stay so loving and positive. But, he was, which helped me a lot.

I reached across his truck seat and hugged him hard. I said I loved him and that I'd see him soon. I told him I had work the next day and would be gone until Thursday, and we talked a bit about my job. Then, I went inside and crashed out. Time with my family was always exhausting.

The next day, when I got to Windemere, Donny and Ed were my shift partners, so that was fun. I liked working with them both. They, strangely, treated me like a woman and would do most of the hard lifting with the boys. That was great for me. When I worked with other staff, which happened whenever Ed needed a day off, or for whatever other reason, I had to be the heavy. That was stressful and scary, and also tiring.

On Tuesday I got a call at the facility. Ed yelled up at me to come get the telephone, which was in the kitchen area. When I got to the phone, it was Miss Carole. I was surprised to hear her voice, but delighted. She had called to tell me that, when the girls had gone out to R Place on Saturday without me, they'd heard about this duo R Place had hired to come perform the following Friday night.

I explained I was working Friday night overnight. I had offered to cover Danny's overnight shift for him that week so he could go on a weekend hunting trip. But, I told Miss Carole that I'd pop into R Place on my way to work to say hi and check out this duo. She said the new bartender had been bragging about it. They were friends of his new boyfriend, supposedly, and he wanted to fill the place for their performance.

The week flew by, though, and I was enjoying the weather we'd been experiencing. With Spring just around the corner, Sudbury was finally warming up. It felt nice to not have to put on so many clothes, and to roll the window down in the car again. I love spring.

Friday came and Smokey called to ask if I was coming tonight. I told her I was working the graveyard shift, but that I'd be popping by, and she was glad. I got my Dykiest shit on, black jeans, a black shirt, a pair of black boots and my brown leather jacket, and left the house for R Place.

It wasn't too packed when I got in. The Dykes were all sitting in the booth at the back, and the duo had set up right in front of the bar, facing the tables. The music played, and this voice echoed though the bar. I walked over and got a beer from Paddy, then headed over to the big table of girls, all smiling, at the back. Miss Carole met me halfway and hugged me hard, like she always did.

"Oh my god, they're good. Just listen," she said. "And she's cute, eh?"

I was greeted by the rest of my buds. I could hear the singing, and they were good. The piano man with her was a funny sort of fellow, I thought.

"What's with the big guy?" I asked Miss Carole.

"Oh, this is a good one. That's her husband!" she blurted.

"What?"

"Yeah, it's her husband. That's what Paddy told us."

I continued to watch them play. The woman played keyboard, and the big guy played the piano and did most of the singing. They were excellent. In fact, the big guy was a killer vocalist and I was blown away when he started to sing. I felt like I was standing in front of Frank Sinatra himself.

"Yes!" I yelled out, clapping my hands high above my head so he could see me. He turned his head slightly and caught my eye. He nodded, acknowledging me, as he sang into his microphone.

I looked over at Miss Carole.

"These two are really good," I said. "I mean, she's cute and sexy, but this guy, wow. This man can sing."

I couldn't get enough of him. And she was cute. But I had to go. I downed my beer and said my goodbyes.

I could see out the corner of my eye that the two people performing could see the ruckus caused by my departure. I felt bad about the interruption, but I hugged all my buds and then headed to work.

The next day, Miss Carole called me at work again, to see how I was doing after my long shift. I said I was fine, and that I was staying to cover another staff shift all day and wouldn't be done until one a.m. that night. She consoled me, although I was fine. She also told me stories about their big night, and the woman who had been playing music. Miss Carole said that they invited her to a

party at another of our friend's, Susan, next Friday. She told me I
needed to ensure I had that night off.

"You invited that straight woman to our party. Why?"

"She's not straight!"

"What? I thought the big guy was her husband?"

"Yeah, well, turns out they are actually divorced and only play
music together now. She's a Dyke."

"Well, well. Doesn't that change everything."

It did, too. I started thinking about that woman a lot more. I hadn't
thought about her much before. I didn't care about her if she was
married and, honestly, she wasn't that good of a singer. I was way
more interested in her husband, musically; he was a killer
performer. I couldn't even remember what she had been doing.
Singing back up? I don't know.

The one thing I immediately thought about was how cute she was,
and that she had been married to this very large man. That was
interesting to me.

Miss Carole told me more about their night at R Place with the
duo, and how the woman, who was named Dawn, had come over
to their table and met them all.

"She actually asked about you," Miss Carole said.

"She asked about me?"

"Yeah. I was right there when she asked, 'Who was that butch
woman in the brown, leather jacket?' We all knew right away she
was talking about you. Smokey yelled out 'Miss Elaineous,' and
then Silver yelled out, 'Yeah. That's my buddy Elaina,' and we all
laughed. Then we told her how well you could sing and that you
were a correctional officer. She seemed very interested, bud. You
need to come Friday."

"Okay, sweetie. I'll make it happen. Thanks for the play-by-play. I love you."

"I love you, too, Miss Elaineous. I'll see you Friday? Have a great week, love."

"You too, Miss Carole."

Friday couldn't come fast enough, but first, I had to get the night off. Normally, I would be off that Sunday, and would go back Monday until Thursday, then be off again. But, I had already told Donny I would cover his Friday nightshift again for him next weekend. He had something else he needed to do. Or maybe he just didn't want to work overnight on a Friday, I don't know. But, I had said I'd cover it, so now I had to cover myself covering it.

I called the newest staff member and bragged about overtime. Then I talked him into taking the overnight shift for me. So, now I had Friday off, and the entire weekend, too, which was nice.

Smokey and Tracey called me Friday afternoon to make sure I would be coming out that night. I had just gotten up, having worked until one a.m. the night before.

"Yeah. I'm coming, for sure. Can I pick you up?"

"That would be great, Miss Elaineous."

So, I did. I went by and grabbed Smokey from her place around eight, and we headed over to Susan's. When we got there, her small apartment was already packed with lesbians. In the kitchen, they were standing and telling stories. In the living room, they were seated and playing caps, or dancing to the Indigo Girls music that was blaring. It was a lesbian den, for sure. We came in and plunked our cooler full of beer down in a corner.

It was a great night, with so many of the girls there, including a few new women I hadn't met yet, as well, which was always fun.

There was a tall woman they called Sergeant. She was stunning, and today if I could think of anyone whose image might help describe her I would say *Game of Thrones'* Brienne of Tarth. She was over six feet tall, with short, blonde hair. She had a beautiful face and smile. She was older, smarter, calmer than the rest of us. She was dating someone else at the party. They had come with a couple of other Dykes I didn't know very well, but it was fun to party with them.

Sergeant was so tall and cute, I immediately had a crush on her and spent most of the earlier part of the night speaking with her. We planned to play squash together, which I thought was cool. I hadn't played before, and when I mentioned that to her as she was telling us she had played ten times that week, she offered to teach me.

Just then, shit started to go down in the kitchen, and we all heard Susan yelling.

"No way, man," she shouted.

A few of us ran into the kitchen. It was a hell of a scene. The room was full of worked-up Dykes and it was like someone had unleashed the hounds. There were men in the doorway, who had heard our party from the street, and came looking to get in on it. Susan, the host, had tried to turn them away and they were giving her a hard time, so I went right to the door to take care of it for her. They were definitely in the wrong place, but didn't think they were. So, I had to convince them of it, and use brute Dyke force to drive the message home that they were not wanted here.

I went after them hard and fierce, like an angry, starving dog. My teeth were glaring and I'm sure I had spit flying out of my mouth I was so agitated. I attacked and then stood my ground in the doorway. The four men all turned to leave, yelling back, "Fucking Dykes!"

It was a bit messy, but I'd gotten rid of them. I was considering taking off down the driveway after them, but that was when she arrived. She had been standing behind all the men at the door, watching the entire throw down.

She walked in and I leaned over into my cooler, looking at her, and pulled out a beer.

"Hey, I'm Elaina. Want a beer?" I said.

"I know," she said. "I'm Dawn. And that was super-hot."

I'd single-handedly scared four grown men from the place. I was kind of glad I hadn't realized she was watching. Who knows what I would have done to show off, being a young and foolish Dyke at the time.

After Dawn came inside, the other women, at least those who had been at R Place the previous weekend, came over to greet her and thank her for coming. It was a bit like having a celebrity arrive at your party. At least, that's how it felt to us.

I returned to partying with Sergeant, Miss Carole, and Smokey in the living room. We were back telling stories to Sergeant and her girlfriend when Dawn came and stood beside me. I looked over at her and she smiled, her big, brown eyes staring me down. Her short, jet-black hair was in a pixie cut, and I couldn't help but to look her up and down. She had on these blue, leather pants she had been wearing at her performance at the bar, and they were hot. I don't think I had ever seen real leather pants before.

The party ran late into the night until it was just Dawn and I, making out on the living room floor until the sun came up. I drove her home to her townhouse in Chelmsford, which was about twenty minutes away, holding her hand the entire drive. I was floating. A night of making out with this gorgeous singer, I was pretty fucking happy with myself. Thrilled, in fact. She liked me and I liked her, and now I was taking her home.

12

SWAN SONG

Dawn and I were instantly an item. In fact, in true lesbian style, it wasn't long before I moved in with her. She was my first lesbian lover and, for a couple of months, I was truly happy.

I continued to work at Windemere. After moving out of my apartment and in with Dawn, I was much farther away from my facility again. It became a chore to go to work. Whenever I was there, I was thinking about Dawn. At first, it was because I was so in love that I couldn't handle leaving her and being away from her for my lengthy shifts, but after a few months, I started hating going to work for other reasons.

What at first seemed like a blissful arrangement, turned volatile and dysfunctional pretty quick. Dawn was doing things while I was at work. When I would get home after my three-day shifts, things always seemed off. Like, the place would look like it had been partied in for three days.

Dawn had a four-year-old daughter when I met her, but I barely ever saw the kid. Even in the two years that we lived together, I barely saw her. She was always with her dad, who lived in the same town. He was the big guy who had been playing with Dawn when I met her. He wasn't just a good singer; he was an incredible father.

I got to know Earnest quite well over the couple of years I was with Dawn. I thought at first that Dawn would eventually give him full custody of the kid, because she wanted alone time for us when I was home. But I realized, after much investigation, that Dawn barely ever had her daughter, even when I was at work. That was because Dawn was up to no good.

After a few months, I got a new vehicle, a Jeep. Dawn and I decided to go on a road trip to Florida, to get away.

I'd been upset for some time by then, not feeling great in the relationship. Dawn was always getting caught with her pants down. She wasn't that smart, although she was a good liar and a skilled manipulator. She got caught at mostly everything she did but always had a way of exploiting my naivety and loyalty, ultimately drawing me back in to her orb. Like, she'd fool around on me, but then my neighbours, or her brothers, or her ex-husband, or her friends would tell me about it. Her own people would tell me. Why? Because they knew I was young, naïve, and being taken for the biggest ride. I think they were all trying to have my back. I believe she was even worse than I ever found out or realized at the time, but others knew.

Our trip to and from Florida was with Dawn's best friend, Tom. It was kind of fun, but also drama-rama while we were down there. We almost got arrested after Dawn and I got into one of our heated fights. She had been flirting with a woman at a bar we were at. And when I say flirting, I mean when I walked outside Dawn was kissing her. I lost my shit. The fact is, Dawn was always doing that. The second my back was turned, she was making out with someone else.

She was a mess, and the trip was messy, too. But, it was on that road trip to Florida when Dawn and Tom discovered that I could really sing.

I had been napping in the backseat for most of the morning and it was finally my turn to drive. I got behind the wheel, Tom was in the back, and Dawn was up front with me. The tunes were blaring on the new Pioneer sound system I had put into my Jeep before we'd left and I started singing at the top of my lungs to some Steve Miller we had playing. I caught Tom's eyes in my rearview mirror and that was that - they started in on me.

They both convinced me that I was a great singer. I mean I knew that I could sing and whenever I cracked my guitar out at parties I got pretty good reviews but this was different. Dawn was so excited by it that the second we got home she started setting up her gear and making a set list. In many ways, the trip to Florida had been another shit show for us, so this was a great distraction for her, to start playing music with me. Ultimately, it would become another form of manipulation but in the meantime she had me learning songs the first day we got home.

I had taken a leave of absence from Windemere right before we left for Florida. I just couldn't handle the job anymore. When I was there, I was too preoccupied, always wondering what Dawn was up to, and who might be at our place and what they might be doing. Though the job had already started to wear on me, she was really the catalyst that saw me leave that job. It's possible, had my first girlfriend been a nice woman with a chill life, that I might well still be in that career, at that facility, even. But I don't know. Probably not, knowing myself the way I do. The correctional system is terribly broken and my ability to negotiate the texture of that life had led to an unhealthy lifestyle.

I found it hard to do what I was supposed to while also caring about each of the boys inside. It was heart-wrenching to see those young boys be so unloved. It hurt me deeply. It was easy to take that leave of absence, and, as it would turn out, I never went back.

After we got home from Florida, we had nothing but time to sing and learn more songs, and we did. We sold drugs to anyone in need to off-set our living expenses. It only took two weeks for us to have a repertoire big enough to play a set somewhere. We had eight songs, and they were tight.

Dawn loved playing with me. She'd play her digital piano, I'd play my guitar, and we'd sing mostly Patsy Cline and other old country songs. That was what I knew at the time, and also what Dawn had been into having played in her country and western duo with her ex-husband for years.

We started by playing at R Place. We'd set up our gear on a Sunday, and all the women came to watch; some men, too, but mostly women. There was another Dyke duo at the time, doing mostly Indigo Girls covers. They were there as well, and we did back-to-back shows at R Place. It was fun and the lesbians loved it. For our second show at R Place, *The Sudbury Star* came and wrote a story about us. It was my first time getting into the newspaper for playing music. But, it wouldn't be the last.

The reporter wrote great things about us, saying that I was a powerhouse vocalist, Dawn was a beautiful piano player, and that we had stunning harmonies. It's hard to explain, but playing music with someone is a very intimate, powerful, and loving thing to do. When you sing a song together with another person, you must be connected. You have to look at them, they look at you. I follow you, you follow me. I play, you play; you play, I play. I stop, you stop. It's all very connected, and you become close, in a different way.

I like to think the music was why I ended up putting up with Dawn so much longer than I should have. I think she knew that getting me to play music with her would extend my stay and keep me around. She had to know I was getting close to my wits' end with her antics. I had been very vocal about my distaste for, displeasure with, and distrust of her. We had blowouts often.

We started to perform bigger shows and learn more songs. After a few months, we learned enough to play an afternoon matinée, which is a two-hour show. We needed two forty-five-minute sets for that, which came out to roughly fifteen to eighteen songs. If I did enough bantering with the crowd, I could always cut that down for us.

Dawn wasn't that much of a talker, or, at least, she didn't speak to the crowds as much as I did. I was kind of the lead. It just ended up that way. She was the experienced player, but I guess she empowered me and when we were in clubs, playing, I kind of just took the reins.

The first clubs we played in, besides R Place, were some of the roughest bars in Sudbury. The country and western bars along Notre Dame Avenue were the spots where we claimed our regular, once-a-month, Sunday matinées status. These rugged bars had never seen two women entertainers, and were intrigued by us up there, we could tell. They would always want to talk to us in between sets. We would lie and say we were friends, or we'd say we were partners, and people would assume we just meant music partners. On the rare occasion we did tell people we were gay, it never turned out well, like either women would hit on us, men would get angry about women hitting on us, or just outright homophobes would ruin our day with their hateful looks or smirks directed at us. So, we learned pretty quickly not to tell anyone. Most people didn't suspect we were gay. In Sudbury, in those rough country bars, people didn't talk about gay, they didn't know about gay, they didn't think about gay.

Men would hit on me and on Dawn, and we'd laugh and carry on playing music. The Park and The National hotels on Notre Dame became our homes for an entire year of Sunday monthly matinées. And the shit we got to witness in those bars was worth a book in itself. They were places filled with poor, uneducated folks, kind enough, but quick to anger and fight, which came with the heavy drinking usually. The messes we would encounter within those crowds were always draining. Sometimes when we'd take a break from playing music and go into the crowd, people would come up to me and say the most fucked up shit. There was always drama. Sometimes they'd ask about Dawn and me, and we'd look at each other and try to figure out whether these were people we could be honest with or not. It was always a crap shoot.

Dawn and I got into some bar fights while playing, too. She was smaller than me, but way tougher. She'd walk up to anyone and cuff them in the mouth. I'm not sure how she got the nerve to do that, but it was something incredible to watch. Of course, there were always repercussions which came in the form of a reciprocated punch. As the bigger one of the two of us, and as someone who is naturally defensive of my loved ones, I often ended up on the receiving end of those repercussions.

A year or so in, I told Dawn I was sick of all the fights and drama, of playing in local country bars, so she started calling around to nearby resorts and offering us up as a duo to entertain guests. It worked. We started playing the resort circuit up around Lake Nipissing and the North Bay area, up through the French River and Noëlville areas, and the other way, nearing Manitoulin Island and Little Current. Now, that I loved.

It was like going on holiday and playing music. The second summer we were together, Dawn and I played the resort circuit almost all summer long. From one end to the other, our female singing duo was a big hit.

We were now playing covers by Reba McEntire, The Judds and Garth Brooks. This was "the north," and people were passionately into country and western music. We'd shock people with our smooth, heartfelt rendition of Garth Brooks' *The Dance* or the rocking, over-the-top version of *The Thunder Rolls* we'd pull off.

I got into it, and our harmonies were on point. Between our loving, fun personalities and our great performances, we were booked all the time. We were becoming very well known around Sudbury and the outskirts, because of the resort gigs all summer.

One resort we played at on the French River was a fine, rich place. I loved it there. We'd be given a cottage, all our meals in the main guest house would be covered, and then we'd be paid a thousand bucks for two full nights of performing.

The resorts liked that we were two women. It was clean and safe, and not rowdy, which resorts liked. They didn't want people getting too raucous, nor did they attract those types of people. They didn't want bands. They wanted solo acts or duos.

The people who booked cabins at these places had money. Some were American, and that would be fun, mostly because they'd tip us in American dollars, and I loved that.

One time, we were playing a weekend at a fancy resort. It was nearly the end of summer. I remember us being happy, yet bewildered, that they'd called to book us that weekend. It was already October. We couldn't understand who would be out in cabins in the cold of October, but when we arrived it all made sense. The resort was sold out to a bunch of American bear hunters who had rented the entire place for their excursion. There were men everywhere, and they had money and were dropping it left and right. We thought it was a sweet scene until later that night during our set.

We started playing at eight p.m., which was right after dinner. The room we were playing in, which was usually filled with tables of couples dining, was now filled with over a hundred men. They were all drunk and rowdy and away from their wives, alone in the woods.

The weekend didn't turn out to be the best plan for us. We played, and the hunters enjoyed us, but it wasn't our music they were enjoying. They were eyeing Dawn all night. I could see it and they weren't trying to hide it. I could tell they didn't know, or wouldn't have thought, we were a gay couple at all.

They started openly hitting on Dawn, but in that sickening, drunk, gross way. We'd be singing and one of them would get the liquid courage up to come up to us mid-song, and he'd stumble into Dawn's keyboard or my mic stand. It happened all night long. Though you would think that getting to the end of the performance would be a relief, we were far from out of the woods. We still had the rest of the evening to survive and the night, in fact, seemed to only get longer and more dangerous.

After we were done playing, the men made a giant bonfire in the open space between the cabins. They were all outside horsing around, being loud, drunk men. There were a lot of them, and we were just the two of us. We had to go by them to get to our cabin, and we of course had to stop to say hi, they wouldn't have allowed us to go by without it.

I was scared, but Dawn wasn't. She walked over and into that circle of men and was over there partying with them all night. Not me. I just couldn't. So, I sat on the outskirts and talked with one of the resort owners, who had come down to watch over stuff. We sat and watched as Dawn maneuvered the crowd, almost like she was trying to hustle them all. She moved among and around them all in that circle like she was pickpocketing. I just sat and watched her.

The men all acted like Dawn was their personal stripper. They kept turning to keep their eyes on her every move, offering her drinks and constantly toasting loudly and up high for everyone to see. I decided it was time for bed.

"I'm out of here," I yelled over, and Dawn came running.

"Chatter, what's wrong?" She and most of the people I knew through her all called me Chatter by then.

"Nothing. I'm exhausted. I want to go to bed. You coming?"

And, she was gone, back into the crowd of men. She would be gone for hours.

I went to our cabin and fell asleep. I woke up at five a.m. to no Dawn. I went outside to see if they were all still by the fire, but there was only one guy outside, passed out on a table. Everyone else was gone. Fuck. Where was Dawn?

I was in a daze tired and hungover. I looked left and right at all the cabins. I could hear noise coming from one of them, so I walked over. I could hear Dawn inside. I could hear her telling a tall tale, as she usually was.

When I walked in, everyone kind of stopped talking. They all looked at me. I looked at Dawn and said, "Are you ready to come to bed yet?"

For a second I had kind of forgotten where I was, and that these guys weren't our friends, that they didn't know we were gay. One of the guys jumped up from his seat.

"What?"

He looked confused. The men were now looking at me like I was trying to ruin their party. I was taking away the only woman in the place, the one they were all trying to fuck. It didn't go well. I was tired and still a little drunk when one of the men said to me, "Go back to bed. She's good here with us."

That made me mad, and I got right in his face.

"Fuck you," I yelled, and the fight was on. Women didn't speak to men that way.

He pushed me and I fell backwards onto the floor. I hit my head on the coffee table on the way down, and I was out. Dawn came over. She rubbed my head and, while she was saying things to me, as i was coming to I could hear the guys all getting rowdy. I heard, "Fucking Dykes," and men getting madder.

Dawn looked me in the eyes.

"Chatter, we gotta get out of here."

I snapped out of it and looked at her, rubbing my head. I let her help me up, and we started for the door to leave, but not before being heavily berated by the men. They were all very angry and called us every nasty name in the book. It scared me, but Dawn got us out of there. She put me in my Jeep, packed our stuff up fast, and we left.

We weren't halfway home before Dawn pulled five hundred dollars American out of her bra to show me.

"Don't worry, Chatter. At least we left with their money," she said.

She was so happy with herself. I immediately looked in the mirror, hoping no one was following us. She had ripped them off in their drunken stupor. Thank god we had gotten out of there. Who knows what they would have done to us if they had caught her.

Not only were we playing music in bars, but we'd be up all night partying after we were done. The party wouldn't end until the wee hours of the morning. It seemed each venue and each party ended up with Dawn and I in a fight, sometimes even physical fights. She would win those. She would win, because I never hit Dawn. Never, not one time. She would hit me, though.

Whenever she'd get sick of me berating her for doing one of the many things she did, always behind my back but always getting caught, I'd lose my shit and we'd get into it. I'd be yelling and she'd be punching, and that was pretty much how it went.

I felt defeated, embarrassed, broken, and like a failure. How the hell did I end up with such a terrible person? She was good at it.

The things I did during my relationship with Dawn, I never

thought I'd do, never imagined I'd ever do, and can hardly today even stomach or believe I did with her. But I did. I was young, stupid, and in love. It was my first love, my first lesbian lover and relationship and I have always been loyal to a fault; I was the perfect target.

Dawn also did a lot of drugs. Well, I did, too. I smoked a lot of weed, and hash oil, but that was it really. I wasn't into the harder stuff yet. We did a lot to secure our smoke, though. I got involved with people I never should have, and did things I never should have. I got incredibly sick from the last adventure we went on in our relationship, an illicit run I mentioned in *Dyke, A Memoir*.

After that, I couldn't take it anymore. I couldn't take her anymore. I had given up my career to be with Dawn and attempt to make us work. I was now selling drugs, singing on weekends in rough bars, and traveling to do things I would never have imagined I'd be doing.

Finally, my friend Silver called me over to her place for a drink. I hadn't seen her in a long time, not since I was hanging with the lesbians before I met Dawn. Silver had actually hooked up with the woman that Dawn had been seeing for a couple of months right before we got together. Silver told me that, in fact, Dawn had still been seeing that woman when we met. She had still been living with the woman the day she brought me home for the first time. During my first visit to her place, she had covered everything up to make it look like she lived alone.

She had quickly dumped the girlfriend. Dawn had kicked her and her little boy out days after she met me. I had been working at Windemere, then, and I hadn't seen any of this. Dawn had lied about all of it. She'd lied the day I met her, and she'd lied every day thereafter.

Silver told me all she knew about Dawn, including the fact that Dawn was having an affair on me now, and had been for some time, with a woman I knew. I knew her because she was always hanging out with Dawn. Dawn had told me she'd helped this girl out of a shitty, abusive relationship, and that was why she was hanging out with her. It was all a lie.

I listened to Silver, then I went home and got in a fight with Dawn. I went back to Silver's defeated. This time, though, she put me in her truck and took me to go get my shit out of Dawn's place, to get away from her for good. And I did.

To this day, I still can't believe all the things I did in that couple of years with Dawn, all of the shit I learned, and had to try to unlearn. I felt so crushed at the time. It had been one hell of a ride with her. All of the lies, the cheating, the drugs, the trips, the hustlers, the thieves. And me, the fool full of regret, although with a lot of new skills.

13
____

TAKE ME TO CHURCH

After the break-up with Dawn, I lived with my friends Jojo and Ed through part of the winter. I worked at a restaurant in downtown Sudbury called Crystal's. Jojo was the cook and I worked with her until the place went bankrupt and closed. In that couple of months though, Jojo taught me how to cook and run a kitchen. When Crystal's closed-up, Jojo convinced me I now had the skills to run any kitchen.

So, I started at a new kitchen, in a strip club where Benny was working as the bar manager during the day. It was a wild place called Porky's. As soon as I got that job, I also got a small apartment downtown, on Beech Street, and slowly started to get my shit back together. Everything was different now, and I was far removed from my life of working at the correctional facility before I met Dawn.

One week, Benny and I both had the same two days off together. He was over at my apartment visiting and smoking joints as we often did back then. We were lying on my bed, shooting the shit.

"Let's take a road trip," Benny suddenly said.

We looked at each other. I leaped up and was filling a duffle bag with clothes before we could change our minds. We dropped by Benny's to grab a few things, then hit Highway 69 to start our way towards Toronto. That was where Benny and I had always wanted to go, where we'd heard the gays had their very own street and village. We were so excited. We hopped in my Jeep, cranked Stevie Nicks and smoked a joint as Sudbury got smaller and smaller in the rearview mirror. It seemed the more distance we put between ourselves and Sudbury, the happier we got.

We drove Highway 69 past Estaire. About an hour later, we were in Burwash, which I was fairly familiar with because of its deep history, having had one of the largest correctional facilities in Canada in the early nineteen-hundreds. It was a town built completely by slave prison labour to house the many correctional officers and staff needed to run the giant institution. It was so remote and far enough from Sudbury that daily commuting was impossible for staff, so they had built an entire town to support the jail. I remember seeing the signs along the highway, when I was a kid, warning motorists not to pick up hitchhikers, that they might be escaped convicts.

We kept going, past the French River, where I'd spent a lot of time as a child, as my family had lived in West Arm, which was very close by.

At the two-hour mark, we were closing in on Parry Sound where I couldn't help but feel triggered by a bad memory of staying in a roadside motel with Dawn the night we had come back from a horrific trip to Jamaica.

Hour three had us going past Barrie and we started talking about Tom and Rondre, a gay couple I knew from Sudbury. They had moved to Barrie not long ago. I knew them both well. Tom was Dawn's best friend, who had come to Florida with us. We were always tight. His boyfriend was cute and funny, and I'd had fun in the past with him, too.

Tom had big, blue, smiling eyes. He always wore a trimmed beard. He had dark, flowing hair and looked a bit like Barry Gibb. Meanwhile, Rondre was young and cute, tall and thin, with jet-black hair that was short but curly. I always thought he looked a bit like Tom Hanks. They were both wild party boys. I mentioned that maybe we could stop to see them on our way home. Of course, Benny was good to go.

Our sights were squarely set on Toronto and it didn't take us long at all to arrive in the big city. We were high and Benny had played DJ all the way down, lining up one great song after another, so time had flown by. Benny was a great DJ and had awesome music. He was a die-hard Fleetwood Mac and Stevie Nicks fanatic, and I learned a lot of their music on that trip.

Putting the cassettes aside for a while, Benny focused on the map and navigated us right down to Church Street, the street we'd heard was full of gays. We weren't let down. The second we hit that street, all we could do was ooh and aah out the windows at all the gays on the sidewalks walking around in broad daylight.

We were so excited. I found a parking lot, and we ditched the Jeep and started out on foot. We were walking around like real tourists, looking up and all around us as we took each step.

I remember this overwhelming feeling, like being showered with love and warmth, as I experienced what it was like to be openly gay out in public on a city street and be surrounded by other openly gay people. The usual fear of being visibly gay in public that I had become accustomed to was supplanted by sheer joy – to see and be seen without an underlying dread. It was transformative, exhilarating, addictive. We were jubilant, like children at a fairground, and we ran up Church Street squealing.

We said hi to every single gay person on the street. It was invigorating to be in a place where being gay was celebrated. At least, that's how it felt on Church Street. We'd come from Sudbury, where you had to hide that you were gay. You could never be out on the street as openly gay. You'd get killed, or beaten up, for sure. Here it was all different.

I felt like I was living in a dream. My cheeks hurt, I was smiling so much. We kept walking down Church, looking into every shop, looking at every single thing. We'd stop and sit on the curb and just people watch. We'd look at queers and then back at each other, then laugh and smile and hug each other. It was like coming home. We both felt it. It was great to experience it with my best friend.

We walked up and down the street a few times until we eventually found a great bar with a window that opened onto the street, overflowing with gay boys hanging out of it. As we approached, some drunk boys catcalled us in. My Benny was a real looker, so it didn't take long for us to meet a bunch of boys. The party was on.

The bar was called Bar 501 and from the open window ledge, I could see drag queens and Dykes and gay boys all over. It was like a carnival of queers. I was beside myself. Benny and I kept laughing. We were having so much fun.

We ended up spending most of the night at 501. We were just having such a fantastic time with all the boys in there. It was a gay men's bar, so we didn't meet any women, but that was fine by me. I was just there to party with Benny and experience everything. The last thing on my mind was hooking up.

I met a couple of gay boys who were instantly friends. We spent all night partying and hugging and telling stories. They kept introducing me as the "big Sudbury Dyke" to other gay guys in the place. They were acting like I was their pet Dyke. They'd buy me drinks, take me into the washroom stalls to do lines, and make sure I always had a stool to sit on. They were taking such good care of me, I thought I might never go home.

That wasn't the case for Benny. By the time midnight rolled around, Benny was on some guy's lap and they were hot and heavy. I, on the other hand, was partying with every guy in the place. We were in the washroom, then hanging off this giant windowsill, yelling at all the people on the street, then up dancing in the open window. It was all so wild and hectic.

I was thinking again how it was like a dream that we could be doing all of this, out in the open. That we were on a major city street in downtown Toronto, the biggest city in our country, and we were all being gay and out. It was a real awakening of sorts. Until I experienced this, I didn't even know it was possible.

In Sudbury, all gays had to hide. Most people weren't openly gay, or out with their families or work friends or anyone. It just wasn't safe. To be in Toronto and so out and in the middle of a street full of other out gay people was empowering. I knew I'd be going back to Sudbury with some hope, that there was a better, bigger existence for gays, outside of our homophobic, redneck city.

It was about one a.m. when Benny came over to me and said he wanted to go to this guy's apartment to hook up. He asked if I would come and wait for him. His new friend was all over me, trying to persuade me to go to his place. I'm sure he figured it was the only thing that could get in the way of him getting what he wanted, which was Benny.

I agreed, and he paid our bill from the night. I thought that was cool. Then we all took off. Weaving in and out of all the gay folk along Church Street, I was walking and watching and grinning in amazement.

We started up in the opposite direction from which Benny and I had come earlier, towards this guy's apartment. We all laughed and stumbled, our arms linked in each others' hurtling into the next ride in what the big gay Church Street theme park had to offer us. The guy's apartment was only a couple of blocks away in a large skyscraper, taller than any building I had ever been in. We got in the elevator and it took us up, up, up, to the fifteenth floor. When we arrived at his place, I was shocked.

We walked in and it was a beautiful apartment. He had art all over. There was a big sword attached to the wall, and there were all kinds of things I had never seen before. The guy made me a drink and said I could have a seat and wait for them in front of this big fireplace. Then he and Benny took off down a hallway and disappeared into his bedroom.

I sat there and finished my drink and within a couple of minutes, I got bored. I started to look around. I looked all over the place. I figured the guy had his hands full, so it was safe for me to snoop around a bit. I opened drawers and looked inside them. I went into his big kitchen and opened his fridge and looked at his food. I walked out onto his balcony and stared down the fifteen stories to the bottom, making myself dizzy and nauseous for a second. In my excitement, I'd forgotten about my fear of heights. I went back inside.

I went over to his bar area. I saw a new bottle of gin on a stand, opened it, and poured myself a glass. It was a drink I was very accustomed to. It had been my mother's drink of choice while I was growing up. So, I had drunk plenty of gin by that point. It went down hot and smooth and flowery, just as I remembered.

I heard the boys and suddenly remembered why I was there. I could hear them talking. I could hear Benny's voice. They must have been done what they were doing. I figured they'd most likely given each other a blow job. I could hear them talking and figured they'd be coming out of the bedroom soon.

I wanted to get back out onto the street. I looked over and saw this bottle of booze on the mantle above the fireplace. I grabbed it and shoved it into my pants, pulling my shirt down over it and drew my big, leather, fringed jacket overtop of it all.

When Benny came out, he had a big grin on his face. I grabbed him and said "Let's go." I started dragging him out of the apartment.

"Thanks!" I said to the guy as I dragged Benny up the hallway towards to elevator. He said goodbye and he and Benny thanked each other as I pulled Benny into the elevator, rushing him.

"Let's go, let's go," I said.

When we got to the bottom floor, the elevator doors opened, and we started for the door exiting the building.

Just as I thought we were out safely, we heard, "Hey!"

We both turned around. It was the guy from upstairs, he had taken the other elevator down, and he was pissed off and heading angrily our way. I looked at Benny.

"Run," I yelled.

Benny looked at me, bewildered. Then he half-rolled his eyes, coming to the realization that I must have done something. He whipped the door open and we ran off, outside and down the building steps. As we were running away, all we could hear was:

"Fucking Dyke, that's my prized Sake!"

"Holy shit," I said. I looked at Benny, and he looked at me.

"What?" Benny looked all confused. So I stopped and pulled the bottle out from where it was tucked under my jacket and showed Benny, and he started to laugh.

"Drop it," he shouted. And I did. I put it down on the front lawn of the building, being careful not to break it. Then we bolted. We could hear the guy still yelling at us.

"You fucking Dyke. This is prized sake!"

"Be glad you got it back, asshole," I yelled back at him.

It had been on display on this fireplace mantle, but I wasn't thinking. I saw a bottle of booze and thought it would come in handy. I would never have thought, or have known to think, that some booze would be "prized."

We ran from the side street back to Church Street, gasping for breath in between giggles, both of us laughing and Benny giving me shit.

"At least I left his sake on the front lawn of his apartment for him. I could have just kept it," I said.

I didn't want fucking sake, anyway. It was the first time I'd ever heard the word, or of the drink. It didn't sound like what I was after, so no loss.

We flagged the first cab we saw and jumped in. We were extremely drunk and happy and I told the cab driver to take us to the biggest bar on Church Street. He agreed and started driving.

We were in the back seat, laughing and carrying on, being our loud and rowdy selves, giggling about the sake, and the guy paying our bill, and Benny getting lucky. As the cab ride went on, we got caught up in our stories, not realizing that the ride had veered off track and was taking longer than a usual run up Church Street. When I looked up, I noticed that we were sitting at a green light. Just sitting there. The car wasn't even moving. The light turned from green to yellow, to red while I watched it.

"Hey! That light was just green," I exclaimed. "What are we doing just sitting here?"

The cab driver had been sitting for I don't know how long at this light, not moving, while we told our stories and had our little party in the back seat. It set me off.

"How long have you been sitting here?" I asked. "The light was green, you motherfucker! Fuck this shit."

I glared over at Benny.

"Get out," I said, and reached over him to open his car door. I shoved him out, tumbling him onto the street. He nearly fell on his face out of the cab. I pushed and shuffled my way across the back seat, to exit after him. I grabbed Benny by the back of his shirt, and we were up and running down the street. We could hear the cabby yelling at us in the distance.

"You haven't paid. I want my money! I'm calling the police."

"You're a fucking crook. Go right ahead," I yelled back.

I pushed Benny along as we made our way back to Church Street. We could still hear the cabby yelling in the distance as we pushed on, not looking back.

I was, however, growing worried that the cops would come looking for us. Between stealing the guy's sake and now this cabbie, I wondered if maybe we were pushing our luck. I most certainly stood out. I was a big, butch Dyke with a fringed leather jacket, the fringe swaying all over as I walked.

It was nearing three a.m. and I was done with this night; we both were. We hadn't eaten since we'd stopped at Burger King in Parry Sound on the way down earlier in the day so we were starving and, we were both still a little paranoid that the cops were after us.

We saw a busy place, so we stopped. It was a pizza joint full of gay boys eating outside. They were eating their pizza slices right out front, sitting or standing on Church Street. You'd buy a single slice and pay two dollars. I'd never seen a pizza place sell only a single slice. Everything seemed new, even the pizza.

I took my jacket off and folded it up. We sat on it on the sidewalk. I figured the cops wouldn't know how to find me without my fringe swinging all over. As we were trying our best to blend in, eating our pizza, I noticed a pay phone across the street, between two buildings.

"Hang on," I told Benny, and ran over.

I looked back at Benny sitting on the curb, eating his piece of pizza and looking over at me. I threw a quarter into the phone. I was going to call Tom, my good friend in Barrie. We were in downtown Toronto, we didn't really have a plan or anywhere to stay, and now I was afraid the cops were going to find us.

I called the operator and asked her to call Tom's number collect for me. To my great surprise, he answered the phone right away and accepted my collect call. That was a bonus. When he answered, he was high as a kite. He told me that he and Rondre had been up doing acid and were thrilled to hear from me.

When I said I was only an hour away, in Toronto, they lost their minds with excitement and begged us to come over. Which, of course, was the best-case scenario for Benny and me at that point. We had nowhere to go or stay, and we didn't feel like sleeping in the Jeep, which was our plan.

I had spent a lot of time with Tom when I was dating Dawn. They had known each other since high school. Between that and the Florida trip only a year ago, Tom and I knew each other well.

I crossed the street back to where Benny was still sitting on the curb. I had been watching him the entire time I was on the phone with Tom. He was surrounded by a couple of boys, of course. They were all chatting him up, and he them.

"Let's go. Buddy," I said.

Benny looked over at me, bewildered.

"Go where, hun?" he asked.

I filled him in on the plan and we started to walk back to the parking lot on the side street where we had left my Jeep. We got the map out and started to figure our way back out of the big city. Thankfully, Benny was a brilliant co-pilot. It took us no time at all to find the Don Valley Parkway and head to the 400 back towards Sudbury.

Benny was thrilled to find out we were going to Tom and Rondre's place, and that the boys were high on acid. He couldn't believe I'd lined it up and that we were driving there after a full day and night of hard partying, but we were. We laughed uproariously as we drove and talked about all the shit we'd gotten into throughout the day, and all the gays we'd met. We were having so much fun. It had been our big, gay adventure, our first time out of Sudbury and into a big city of gays together, both of us gay. Paranoid escape aside, it was dreamy.

As I drove us towards Barrie, the stories of our night in Toronto kept swirling between us. I wasn't scared anymore at all. I wasn't thinking about anything other than getting us out of Toronto and to Barrie to find the boys. I was on a mission, and dragging Benny with me. Nothing new there.

We drove the 400 to Barrie, and, as we exited into the city, I couldn't wait to see my friends and introduce them officially to Benny, and tell them about our wild twelve hours in Toronto.

14

BARRIE OR BUSTED

When we arrived at Tom and Rondre's, they were both standing at the front window of the house they were renting, waiting for us. As we pulled up, we saw them and started laughing. The boys were waving their arms, and you could tell they were delighted we had arrived.

We pulled into their driveway and parked, and they both ran out to greet us. It was hugs all around as Rondre met my Benny and Tom was reunited with both of us, and took us inside. It was nearing five a.m., but you would have thought it was still midnight, because they started opening beers for us and we all started the party up once again.

Benny asked if they had a stereo. Rondre pulled out his boom box and Benny slipped his Fleetwood Mac *Rumours* tape into it and winked at me.

"Stevie is in the house! Party on," Benny shouted over the music.

Benny felt comfortable right away and we all hit it off as if we'd all known each other for years, when it was mainly Tom and I who knew each other, Benny knew of Tom and Tom knew of Benny, but they hadn't gotten to know each other. I had only met Rondre twice before this. I was so delighted to be there with them, though. It was nice to see Tom.

It had been a while now since we'd both left Dawn. For me, it had been the breakup and ending our playing music together, and for Tom it had simply been getting away from her. He had been her best friend for years, but she had used him terribly, making him the fall guy for most of her dirty deeds. He had been her partner in crime, until Rondre.

Of course, Dawn didn't like Rondre. The dynamics were all fucked up for her and she got frustrated. Instead of pulling them in together, she alienated them both. She was pulling Tom one way and Rondre the other. Tom realized he couldn't have both of them in his world. He chose love. That meant his relationship with Dawn soured. If she couldn't control his every move, she wasn't happy. She couldn't have a relationship she wasn't in control of.

The entire time I had known her and Tom, I had seen her manipulate him and use him. Hell, when her kid was born, Dawn even told people, and had him corroborate, that Tom was the father, to cover up who the father really was. Then, when it was convenient for her, she made up that it was another man, the big guy she was with. But, he also wasn't the real father.

That was Dawn. Tom and I had both needed to get away from her clutches. Thankfully, we did. Now, with both of us far away from her and into our new lives, it felt special for us both to connect in this way, like we had lived through something very messed up. And we had.

We partied with the boys all morning and told them our adventures from the last twenty-four hours starting with the spontaneous road trip decision in my apartment, to driving to Toronto, and all of the escapades in the big gay festival that is Church Street. They laughed and drank and told us stories, too. They'd been in Barrie only a couple of months, but had gotten to know a few people there. They certainly had their own stories to share.

We were all going on and on, laughing and telling stories. Finally, around seven a.m. I started to feel dizzy, and nodded off while the boys were partying around me. I fell into a deep sleep, right there on their couch. When I woke up, I was alone in the living room. I had a blanket over me and a pillow under my head. It was comfy. I rolled over and went back in for a couple more hours. I was half wondering where Benny was, but I figured he must have found a place to crash, too. I was out of it, and fell back into a deep slumber.

When I finally woke up around noon, the boys had beaten me to it and were up making us all breakfast in the kitchen. I got up, went to the washroom, cleaned myself up a bit and then joined them.

The party was back on. They hadn't slept at all. What they had done was have a threesome with Benny. They were all laughter and smiles. Tom and Rondre told me how much they loved Benny. I was pleased they were all getting along so well and that they'd had so much fun while I was catching some Z's. But, now the party was back on for me, too. I'd gotten some rest, so I was good to go.

"Where's the acid, boys?" I asked. I looked over at Benny and mouthed, "One more day?"

"Whatever you say, hun," he laughed.

And, that was that. We were staying another day with the boys in Barrie.

I decided to go for a drive with Tom to get some beer in downtown Barrie. We stopped in at a corner store for some smokes. It turned out that Tom knew the woman behind the counter, so we spoke with her for a bit. Tom introduced us. Her name was Shelley. She was cool and open and fun. I could just tell, she was so bubbly and smiley. Tom mentioned she was straight.

I looked at him and winked, "Straight to bed."

We both laughed. When Tom mentioned to her that we were partying at his place, she said she'd pop by after work, which made me smile. Another woman around. Awesome.

We got our beer and drove back to the apartment. When we walked in, Benny and Rondre were making out again, so Tom just jumped in. I continued to the kitchen to put the beer into the fridge and make myself a baloney sandwich.

I had gotten a loaf of bread and pack of baloney at the store and was making sandwiches for all the boys, too. I made an entire loaf of baloney sandwiches, using their margarine and mustard. The boys didn't take long. I guess they were mostly done when Tom arrived into the sex mix. They joined me in the kitchen, where we had coffee and sandwiches.

It was that open with me around gay men in those days. I can honestly say that I've witnessed more gay male sex right in front of me than any other kind of sex. I'm not sure why they were always so relaxed around me, but I got to see how they did it a few times, and I was blown away each encounter. I love what my eyes have seen, and I love that I had the opportunity to experience these things.

Our sandwiches done, the party was back in motion. Tom put on some tunes, and Rondre passed both Benny and me a hit of acid. We looked at each other.

"Here we go again, bud," I said.

We swallowed the acid, and the night took off like a jet from there.

We partied, we drank beers, we sang songs at the top of our lungs, because Tom always wanted to hear me sing. I was all fucked up and singing at the top of my lungs for him and Benny, my other biggest fan. I sang Stevie Nicks so loud that day.

"Just like the white-winged dove, sings a song sounds like she's singin' Oooo, baby, ooo, I say ooo."

I sang and sang.

Then Shelley showed up. We were all such a mess, high on acid and drinking, but she came in like she'd been there the entire time. She grabbed a beer out of the fridge and came to dance and sing with me in the living room.

We partied all night with Shelley. She was fun. Tom had said so, and he was right. He'd mentioned in the car on our way home that she was straight but completely open to the gays, and that she wanted a lesbian encounter. Well, she was getting her lesbian encounter, alright. Since I already knew she was interested, I gave her lots of attention. I'd say I downright seduced her.

The night was fun and, when the boys all took off into the other room in the wee morning to make out, Shelley and I rolled on the floor and did our own making out. We kissed and I took her pants off and went down on her. She howled like a dog in heat. When I made her cum, she was thrilled.

"Yes, yes, I knew it," she yelled.

I started laughing.

"Knew what?"

"I knew sex with a woman would be awesome!"

Now I started laughing harder. She went on to explain that she hadn't had an orgasm in her life before tonight. She was sure of it. She said she liked sex with men, but she never got off with them. It was always over too fast. I laughed and explained a woman knows a woman's body, just like a man knows a man's body.

"That's why they are having so much fun in there." I pointed toward the room to which the boys had all escaped.

She liked my explanation. I could see her thinking about what I was saying. It was nice to be with her, we lay in each other's arms until the boys came back out, all disheveled and worn but glowing, in the morning. Shelley and I had passed out for a couple of hours before waking up. We were just lying there, talking, when the boys came out.

It was such a fun trip. We were all still high for hours, while we chatted and gossiped and laughed through the morning.

I finally looked at Benny in that way. It was close to ten a.m. and Shelley was talking about leaving, since she started work at noon and wanted to get home and shower first. That was when I stood up and decided it was time for us to head home, too.

"We have to work tomorrow, Benny. We've still got to get home, and I've got so much shit to do. Let's start back to the Nickel, shall we?"

The party was over and all I could think about now was getting us back to Sudbury and getting some real rest before we both had to go back to work the next morning. I opened the kitchen at seven a.m. at Porky's, and Benny needed to be there for ten a.m., when the restaurant opened. We were still a mess, but I had at least gotten a couple of hours of sleep with Shelley on the floor, and I felt good enough to drive.

Shelley got up, came to me, and kissed my mouth. She leaned over and whispered in my ear, "I'll never forget you. Thanks for the great night."

I hugged her hard. She was nice, and beautiful, and I'd had fun with her.

The boys said goodbye, and she was gone. Now it was Benny's and my turn to pack our shit up and head out. I could see Tom start to get sad that we were leaving. I know he'd had as much fun as Benny and I had. It was nice to reconnect after a year or so of both of us getting away from Dawn.

The boys were far away in Barrie, with only very few friends. They'd left their families and communities to get away from it all. They hoped they could get jobs locally in Barrie and stay away from the hardness and straightness of Sudbury.

When I hugged Tom, it was extra-long. I thanked him for taking us in. It had helped us get away from Toronto when we'd needed to, and given us a safe place to land. I thanked him for the great partying and the warm home they'd provided for us to hang in for a couple of days. I couldn't thank him enough. We had both survived Dawn, and that was a blessing we were both very aware of. It bonded us even deeper.

The boys hugged Benny, and they all gushed over the great time they'd had together. We finally jumped in my Jeep, and we were off. Back to Highway 69, and headed home to Sudbury. It would only take us about three and a half hours, I had estimated. Benny slept for most of the drive. He was pooped. I don't think those boys got any sleep in that bedroom.

I was happy Benny got to experience so much gayness on our trip. Hell, he'd hooked up with three different guys, and had a threesome. That was a big, gay adventure for sure.

As I looked over at Benny's sleeping face while I drove, I couldn't help but remember him as an eleven-year-old kid with his hand in a chip bag and his teeth full of sour cream and onion chips. How I had loved him so much then, and how I loved him so much more now. How we had grown up together and how we'd never known we were both gay. How we were now together again, and gay together, and experiencing what it was to be gay, together. I got teary then, but I kept my eyes on the road, and headed gayly forward to Sudbury.

I felt so content, loved and calm, softly, singing along to Christine McVie as she soothed us with her *Songbird*, a favourite ballad on our favourite album, *Rumours*, by Fleetwood Mac. A beautiful serenade, it was placed right in between my two favourite songs on that album, the party anthem *Go Your Own Way*, and the song I would later name my full band after, *The Chain*.

I sang the entire album, while Benny slept and I watched over him. It had been a special getaway with my best friend, one that we have never forgotten since, or ever will.

15

——————

D BAR

Porky's Roadhouse, as we liked to call it, was the same ol', same ol' when we got back to work Tuesday morning. The regulars were all sitting around waiting for their free bowl of soup, which the owner would dish out so they'd spy for him. Essentially, anything that happened around that place the owner knew about, because he had his little spies everywhere. All the homeless, broken folks he'd feed free soup to on the daily.

Benny worked the bar and I was in the kitchen. After our weekend of sleepless nights and gayventures we were both deeply hurting. We hadn't had any time at all to recover from our debauchery, and we were slow going. At one point, I walked out of my kitchen and of course heard Benny telling stories about our Toronto trip. I could see their eyes widening as Benny recanted the ins and outs of our exploits.

Benny also worked at D-Bar, the newest gay bar in town. It opened shortly after R Place closed. It was located in the basement of Sudbury's old city hall building, on Cedar Street, right downtown. Benny worked there at night. Between jobs he'd smoke a few joints and then head into D-Bar for his shift where he'd open the bar at seven p.m., and stay until it closed at two a.m. This was the usual closing time unless, of course, Benny was planning one of his male stripper nights, which were always hot nights around D-Bar. The boys loved it and there were no women allowed. Well, almost no women, wink, wink.

I seem to have always been allowed in the men's spaces. I'm quite sure, looking back at it, that it was because I egged them all on. I was never shocked or turned off or prudish about anything I ever saw.

Tuesday nights were normally slow in Sudbury, but not tonight. My friend Jude lived in the apartment above Porky's, and went to Laurentian University. She was also my part-time salad girl on Fridays. Her roommates came down to Porky's early in the day to tell us they'd be going out after school tonight. So, we knew the party would be on.

I was home, catching up on some much-needed rest before heading back out to the bar later that night. Miss Carole had called and left a message on my machine saying she'd be in town all week and wanted to go out tonight. She worked seven days on and seven days off with CN. I missed hanging with her like we used to before she started with the tracks. Not as much as I missed Smokey, though. She had moved to London, Ontario, to be with Tracey, who had been transferred to another job a few months back.

Things were a bit different now than before I was with Dawn, I was also very different. I used to want to be in a relationship then, and now I totally didn't. I wanted to be single and play the field. After what I went through with Dawn, I was now very wary of relationships. My first relationship had been harrowing and I would still wake up in hot sweats thinking about her and everything I had done while I was with her.

I phoned Miss Carole's parents' place, where I knew she'd be staying while off and in Sudbury for the week. Her folks still lived in Azilda, a little town just outside of Sudbury, about a fifteen-minute drive from the downtown. Miss Carole was outside mowing the lawn for her parents when I called. I got her sweet mother on the phone. She was very French, and I always stumbled when speaking to her, but I would slowly explain I was looking for Miss Carole. Her mother would recognize my voice right away and knew what I was after, regardless, so she'd call after Miss Carole for me. She'd say the same thing every time:

"Ma chérie, Mademoiselle Martín est au téléphone."

Today, Miss Carole came to the phone and we made plans to meet up with Benny at D-Bar later. I told her I'd come and pick her up. That made her happy, because she loved my Jeep. She would always insist on taking the top off and riding in it as a convertible. Miss Carole enjoyed it so much and I'd often lend it to her to go on dates when she was in town, since she didn't have a vehicle of her own, yet.

I went out to Azilda to get her, then we headed back downtown to D-Bar to see Benny. Of course, he was all smiles and his happy self when we walked in.

"Hey, ladies. How're my favourite lesbians?"

We laughed and grabbed stools at the bar with him. It was still fairly quiet as he'd just opened up, and it was a Tuesday. That said, Miss Carole had called a lot of the girls to come out and party with us so, one after another, the girls all rolled in, and the night revved up, Fleetwood Mac blaring through the sound system as Dykes piled onto the dance floor.

Marty the drag queen was there, and in full drag. She was seven feet tall in her heels. We loved partying with Marty; she was such a wild girl.

Miss Carole was propped at the bar, in deep conversation with Benny, when I came off the dance floor with some Dykes and headed over to grab another beer. They both were smiling at me in a weird way.

"You two look like you're up to trouble," I said. "What's up?"

"We think you should play a solo show here, darlin'." Benny piped up.

Then Miss Carole started going on and on.

"Okay, yes. My next full week off is in two weeks, and I'd love to bring my sister and a woman I work with at CN and—"

"Hey, you two. I haven't played since Dawn."

"Who cares, get back on the horse darlin'," said Benny. "We'll all be here cheering you on. You've got nothing to worry about."

But, to me, I did have lots to worry about. I hadn't played much before Dawn. I was an amateur. Of course, now, after having played music hundreds of times to various crowds with Dawn for a couple of years, I was way more seasoned. But I had always played with her. I was nervous thinking about playing by myself again. It had been so long.

Benny and Miss Carole could see that I was scared. They both showered me with beautiful words and encouragement and before the night was over, they had picked a date for my first solo gig. It would be in two weeks, when Miss Carole was home again.

Benny didn't waste any time and wrote it on his promotion chalkboard right away. When the Dykes came to the bar from the dance floor to grab drinks, he got busy spreading the word, getting them all to promise they'd be in attendance.

That was Benny. He was my secret manager, publicist, and marketer in those early years. He was so enthusiastic, and convincing, too. It was a joy to have him be so supportive and protective of me. My childhood sweetheart, turned best friend, turned manager.

Even though it was only Tuesday, the girls were all into the party and ensured Miss Carole made up for her week away at work. When it was time to close, Benny was exhausted. I could see it in his eyes. He hadn't rested much since our return from Toronto. He needed to go home. My Benny was pooped.

Miss Carole had other plans, though, and had already convinced most of the ladies to join us. We were going to go to the beach and hang out. She wanted to go for a swim. I was always game for anything, so thought it was a great idea.

We all packed into my Jeep and, at Miss Carole's request, took the top off. Even Marty the drag queen came with us. It was me and Miss Carole in the front, and two other Dykes in the back with Marty. All I could see in my rearview mirror was billowing red material from Marty's flowing gown, and her curly dark hair flapping in the wind. When in drag, Marty used his own hair, because he had a wild, long, curly head of hair.

We cranked the Stevie Nicks on my car stereo, and Miss Carole and everyone, myself included, sang at the top of our lungs to every word until we got to the lake.

It was only about a fifteen-minute drive to get to this private beach I knew at Kelly Lake. It wasn't necessarily private, but it was always empty when I went there. It was remote and, bound to be deserted at three in the morning, so I assumed we'd have the place to ourselves.

I could have taken them to all kinds of beaches, since Sudbury is full of them, but I figured Kelly Lake would be the most private for a bunch of Dykes and a drag queen to swim at in the wee hours of the morning. I also knew all the other beaches had security at them, where this one didn't.

Sudbury is the city in Canada with the most freshwater lakes within its boundaries—three hundred and thirty, to be exact.

We arrived at Kelly Lake and I pulled off the road. There was a small kind of parking area, mostly just bare sand, but a space by the water where you could park a vehicle.

Kelly Lake wasn't a public beach per se; it was just a place I had gone swimming a few times when I was a kid, with my papere. He liked to take us there, because it was bright blue, and surrounded by beautiful rocks, and had a slow, sandy incline into the water. But mostly, I think it was because it was one of the quietest, least attended beaches in Sudbury. I don't remember anyone ever being there when I was there before.

There were five of us in my Jeep, and another two cars of Dykes had followed behind. A swath of lesbians was pouring out of those cars now, too.

We all sat along the water, on the sand, and laughed and told stories and did our usual carrying on. Miss Carole soon had her pants and shirt off. She was naked, walking into the water up to her knees. With the moon shining above her as she entered, she looked back at me.

"You said you'd come swimming with me, Miss Elaineous," she called.

"Indeed, I did, honey."

I took off my pants and shirt and bra, and walked into the water after her. The other girls were poking their fingers into the water, and remarking how cold it was, and how they were definitely not going in. But, Miss Carole was already treading water, in far enough that the water would be above her head, and I wasn't going to let her down.

I swam out to her, and she wrapped herself around me. We floated there under the moon, holding each other's naked bodies closely for warmth, and listened to the women talking on the shoreline. I would swirl us around in the water and she'd smile.

"I love you," she said over and over again as I swirled her round and round.

Miss Carole was so intense, and I'll admit that intensity was addictive for me. I'm also very intense, and I appreciate someone who knows how to express their feelings with conviction and passion. That was Miss Carole. She was holding on to me so tightly, and nose-to-nose she told me how much she loved me, and how happy she was that we were in each other's lives. We were having one of our regular mushy moments.

Then a car pulled up. We could hear it revving its engine. It had its high beams on and we were all blinded by the light. It pulled up beside our vehicles. Its engine and lights turned off. We all thought it must be someone else from D-Bar coming to join us. But that didn't make sense, because everyone we were with at D-Bar was already here.

A car full of straight men got out. There were three of them, but it felt like a carload. They were drunk and looking to party with some women. It didn't take long for things to head south, I'll tell ya. I was still holding onto Miss Carole in the water when I heard Silver say, "Hey man, we're not into partying with you. We're just here having a nice time together. We don't want any trouble."

My guard had gone up instantly. I was frustrated that I was a ways out in the water, with Miss Carole wrapped around me, as these guys pulled in. I could hear the women trying further to talk them out of staying.

Then I heard, "Hey, want some company out there?"

One of the men was looking out at Miss Carole and me in the water. Miss Carole pulled me close to her and spoke in my ear.

"Are we going to be okay, Miss Elaineous?"

"We sure fucking are, babe. But I have to go in right now. You wait here and I'll come back out in a second."

I turned to the shoreline and started wading my way back so I could take care of this. I could tell everyone was nervous and scared. I could see it in their body language, they had all gotten up on their feet now, no longer sitting relaxed on shore. I could see it in their faces as my naked body arrived back at the shore. I was staring directly at the man who was doing all the talking, and as I walked up to him , I didn't take my glare from him.

As I got to the shoreline, one of the girls had my pants and shirt and passed them to me and I quickly pulled them over myself. Then I hear one of the women groan.

"Ewww. What the fuck?" she cried out.

One of the guys had decided he was joining the party, had dropped his pants and was making a move toward the water. I could hear all the women groan and moan in disgust.

"I like skinny dipping," the guy said as he started for the water, towards Miss Carole, his cock swinging as he staggered forward drunkenly.

I hurriedly pulled my pants up and made my way over to intercept him, there was no way I was going to let him anywhere near her. I was in full defense mode – I have always been able to quickly pull out of celebration and into survival mode and I was increasingly growing upset, having had our beautiful night interrupted and feeling the prick of homophobic violence threatening our warm revelry.

I came and stood right in front of him as he walked down the sand to the water.

"Hey, what's the matter with you?" I said. "You can't tell we don't want you here? You can't see that no one here wants to swim with you or have anything to do with you?"

"Fuck you, you fucking Dyke! You can suck my big dick, bitch!"

That's when I clocked him, hard.

You see, I'd already been to this rodeo a few times before. The straight men show up, call us fucking Dykes, then beat us up. And I'd always ended up getting hit in the face or hurt. I guess after getting hit in the face a few times, you get harder, tougher, less afraid of getting hit.

When Ed had trained me at the facility, he'd told me once, when a man comes up to you to start trouble, hit him as hard as you can, right in the nose. That'll slow things down so you can either escape or start kicking him in the balls.

Hit or be hit was how he'd described it. Since you know it's coming, why wait for it? Take control.

I heard Ed in my head as I pulled back my fist and smashed the guy's face with it. Oh, I was setting the pace, alright. He hit the sand hard. His friends jumped in and came at me, and that's when I lost my shit.

Miss Carole told me later that I looked like a wild animal, and sounded like one, too. I get very aggressive when someone else is being hurt, or myself, even. I hate hurting, and it seemed to happen all the time in those days at the hands of angry, straight, homophobic men. I lost it.

The naked guy's friend came over and I quickly turned and kicked him so hard in the balls that he hit the sand, too. Then the third guy came over. He looked at me and I looked at him, my eyes wild like I was going to kill him. I might have even said so.

"I'm good," he said. "Sorry. Let me get them out of here."

"Yeah, get them the fuck out of here. Great idea," Silver yelled from behind me.

I was still in a fighting position though, ready to lose more teeth if I had to. Miss Carole had made her way out of the water and came up right behind me. She wrapped her naked body around me from behind. Her arms were around my neck, and her face was next to mine as she whispered in my ear, "My hero."

That guy did got his friends into their car. As they took off, they yelled "Fucking Dykes" a million times out their windows. They also screamed one other thing that most certainly got our attention:

"We're coming back, Dykes, and you'll be sorry."

That was enough for me. I believed them and quickly started getting everyone up and into their cars and my Jeep. It was time to go, and we got out of there without a minute to spare.

Although our night got cut short by our rude intruders, Miss Carole and I would both refer many times to that evening, to floating together. Just her and I under the moon and stars, wrapped in each other's arms together. That twenty minutes was just ours, and would be forever.

16

SAULT STE. MARIE GIRLS JUST WANT TO HAVE FUN

There was a big lesbian outdoor camping party coming up in Sault Ste. Marie. Miss Carole had heard about it from a lesbian she'd started dating who had recently moved to Sudbury from the Sault.

Miss Carole called me up one night while I was having dinner - she knew that was the best time of day to catch me at home. She was up north on the rails with CN, and called me from one of their train phones. She told me that Trina, the woman she was dating, had invited her and some friends to the party in the Sault, next weekend. Miss Carole had the weekend off and was coming home, and she wondered if I'd be interested in going to the lesbian camping weekend, and driving my Jeep with a couple of girls.

I was, of course, very into the idea. We hardly ever got out of Sudbury, and what better destination than lesbian camping! I also didn't get to meet new women or much, since our community was so damn small and we all knew each other.

In a small community with only a handful of openly out lesbians, that was the way it was. I wasn't into dating my friends' exes, though, ever. That made it hard for me to meet lesbians in Sudbury as everyone was someone's ex. I'm pretty sure that's why I was always hooking up with straight women. I most definitely slept with more straight women than i did lesbians back then.

Miss Carole told me she'd be home Friday around noon. She asked if it would be okay for us to leave Friday after Trina was done school, around six p.m. I said that would be fine. It would take us about three hours to get to the Sault, so we'd pull into the party around nine p.m., which sounded perfect. Fashionably late, even. Miss Carole told me she'd pay for the weekend and finalize our plans with the girls from the Sault.

There were multiple cabins at the campground, and people could rent a cabin or pitch a tent. Miss Carole was making good money working with CN, so she was willing to pay for the cabin we were going to share. I'd cover gas and drive. It was a great arrangement, I thought. Trina would be buying the booze. It was all even-steven.

As luck would have it, Smokey happened to be in town that weekend. She'd called me earlier in the week to let me know. I was so happy. I had missed Smokey so much. She stayed at my place and we hung out all week whenever I wasn't working. Come Friday, we hadn't told Miss Carole yet that Smokey was in town. I thought it would be a fantastic surprise. And I was right; it was.

When Friday rolled around, Smokey and I hung out all day, then packed our shit up. I packed my guitar, of course, and got my new cooler out of the closet. I sat down and pre-rolled a dozen joints, for the ride and so I'd have some ready when we arrived. We packed everything, then stopped in at Benny's on the way to Azilda to get Miss Carole. It was still early. We had some time to kill, and Benny didn't start work until seven at D-Bar, so I knew he'd be home.

He was thrilled to see us, of course. Benny loved Smokey, too. They got along great. It seemed then, and still does today, that my good friends all get along great together. Birds of a feather?

Benny rolled a joint from his little *sacoche*, a small, cloth purse, about the size of your open hand. "Sacoche" is a French term for small purse. Benny's had a little zipper, was made of thick cotton and had a funky, tie-dye hippie pattern. It was where he kept his pot and papers, or his oil and pin. He always had his *sachoche* with him, and we'd always remark on it. I loved the word.

We laughed hard with Benny over a joint and some coffee he'd made us. We told him about the big lesbian weekend we were about to embark on, and his crass, jokey reactions made us laugh. Benny is a comedian. Seriously, he can make you laugh so hard you will hurt. He was imagining possible scenarios for our weekend, making up funny stories about me or Smokey or Miss Carole, and they were hilarious.

I could tell Benny wished he was coming with us, if only to be a fly on the wall and see all the lesbians in their natural habitat. I could also tell he was a bit sore that we'd be gone all weekend and wouldn't be visiting him at D-Bar, which we always did, especially when Miss Carole was home from CN.

We said our goodbyes and headed for Azilda, which was just up the highway from where Benny lived in downtown Sudbury. We drove over to Miss Carole's parents' house, where she had arrived earlier. She was outside with her dad when we got there. He was working on a car in the driveway. She ran over and hugged us both, and was surprised and excited to see Smokey. I asked her where Trina was, because I didn't see her.

"She's already out there," she said. "She left yesterday."

"So, it's just you, me, and Smokey on the trip up?"

"Fuck, yeah!"

Oh my god, that made me so happy. Miss Carole had assumed it would be just her and me, which would have been fun, but now it was her and me and Smokey, which was over the top. The three of us were like three peas in a pod; you couldn't get in between us. We were loyal and solid as glue.

We packed Miss Carole's stuff into the back of the Jeep. Smokey got into the back seat, gave the front to Miss Carole and we cranked the tunes. Fleetwood Mac and Concrete Blonde were at the top of our listening list, and we had just been introduced to The Cranberries, so they made the rotation. I was also listening to Weeping Tile, a new Ontario band I had recently heard of. I had gotten a cassette of theirs and was in love with it. I sang out all the songs. I looked in the rearview and saw Smokey looking back at me, a giant smile on her face. Miss Carole either had her hand on my lap or was rubbing my arm, almost the entire way, while I drove. This was my family, and we were on a family vacation. I was deliriously happy.

We couldn't wait to get there. After some wrong turns into Sault Ste. Marie, and after some great directions from an old guy at a gas station, we finally made it to the campsite. When we pulled in, we could see immediately that the place was crawling with lesbians. Everywhere we looked, lesbians! We got out and walked around between the little tents pitched all over. Between some of the cabins, we could see a big flame. We would later find the giant fire on the beach.

Trina was there waiting for us and eager to show us to our cabin. I parked the Jeep, then threw my keys through the cabin's open door. That was me being cheeky, and making it very known that I was done driving for the weekend. Trina came over and I met her for what was only the second time. She was fine, albeit a little snobby.

Trina was very good-looking, but more in a handsome way than a feminine way. I wasn't attracted to her at all, but her attitude is really what turned me off. Don't get me wrong. She was very nice to me, but she had this overall smugness to her that I could later tell came from being rich. That kind of privilege made me sick, and I guess I kind of held it secretly against her.

The moment I saw her and Miss Carole kissing, I became thankful that Trina had gone on ahead of us and not come with us in the Jeep. I could imagine them in the back seat, and that made me nauseous.

We unloaded the Jeep and brought the cooler, our bags, and my guitar into the cabin we were sharing. I picked the top bunk and Smokey took the bottom. Miss Carole and Trina took the single bed against the wall. We pulled out handfuls of beers. Trina was going to give us a tour of the place in the dark and show us around a bit.

"Let's go to the big fire," said Miss Carole. "Bring your guitar, Miss Elaineous!"

Miss Carole started walking, the cooler in her hands. She was strong as a bull. Smokey already had my guitar in her hand, and I had my fanny pack full of joints and cigarettes. We followed Miss Carole and Trina down this path to the big fire, passing lesbian after lesbian on our way. We said hi to each of them, especially Smokey and I. Smokey was newly single, having recently broken up with Tracey, and we were damned if we weren't going to each hook up with a Sault Ste. Marie girl tonight. We had a bet on who'd hook up first. I honestly thought Smokey would win. I wasn't really in the mood to hook up, or, at least, it wasn't on my mind as much as it was on Smokey's. She needed help getting over Tracey. The end of that relationship was hard on Smokey, and she was ready to have a distraction from it all. I just wanted to party with my buddies; that was my priority.

When we got down to the beach, the sand gave way under our feet. We walked over to the fire, where about twenty lesbians were all sitting and standing around. There were a couple of big, butch Dykes who were the obvious fire keepers. They were doing a great job. The flames were high and, with the light coming off of the fire, you could see everyone's faces quite well.

The jamming was well underway, with, of course, the Indigo Girls being played and sung by all the girls. In those days, you could hardly call it a lesbian party if at least one person didn't crack out a guitar and start singing *Closer to Fine*.

I hadn't ever been into them. I would later in my life open up for the Indigo Girls with my band at a big show in Ottawa, but that would be many years later. At this point, it made me roll my eyes. I'd much rather have been rocking out to Fleetwood Mac, but I never said anything. It would have been sacrilegious to do so and I wasn't here to offend the lesbian sensibilities. The Indigo Girls were like Elvis Presley for lesbians at the time.

"How long 'til my soul gets it right?" All the lesbians sang to each word of every song.

Smokey and I cheered with our beers and stood back, watching and laughing together, making up little stories about each funny thing we saw. It felt so darn good to be out of Sudbury and with all these strangers, who were also gay, in another city. We were happy, indeed. What a great idea, I thought.

One beer, two beers, three beers, four …. The party was hopping, and so were we. Miss Carole jumped up from her seat on the sand between songs at one point.

"Hi, I'm Carole," she said to the entire group. "I'm here from Sudbury with my best friends and I would like you all to hear my friend Miss Elaineous sing. She's really good!"

All the women were like, what? And I heard many of them saying, "Let's hear her. Where is she?"

Smokey grabbed my guitar case. She laid it down and opened it up so fast I didn't have time to think as she passed it to me. Now, I'd had a few drinks already and was high. The party was on in my head, and I was bored with all these Indigo Girls songs. So, I decided to pull out a short medley of Steve Miller songs that Dawn and I had made a mash up of. I swung my guitar around my neck and started with *Take the Money and Run.*

I shit you not. The second I started to play, the lesbians, who had all been seated, jumped up and were yelling. They started dancing in the sand right away. The real party had just begun.

I rolled into *Rock'n Me.* I made it an extended version that probably went on for about ten minutes. They all kept dancing and howling. Then I started playing some Fleetwood Mac and the women were beyond excited. I'll be honest. I felt like a superstar in that moment. I had turned this party up something fierce. The party matched the bonfire now.

I started chomping on my strings and rocking out.

"Loving you wasn't the right thing to do. How can I ever change things that I feel? If I could, baby, I'd give you my world. How can I, if you won't take it from me? You can go your own way."

The women all sang along with the chorus. Everyone knew Fleetwood Mac, if only from the radio, but these were party songs, and we brought the party. I just kept playing and belting them out. In fact, the women were all belting the songs out, too. It helped that I didn't have to sing alone. A couple of women had their guitars, too, and started playing along with me, following my chords, and it sounded so much bigger.

I played for about thirty minutes. I decided to end my little set with a hot number and pulled out my acoustic version of George Michael's *Never Gonna Dance Again*> The women went berserk.

When that song was done, I stopped but the chorus of women kept on. When they finally stopped singing, I pulled my guitar off of me, and handed it back to Smokey, who was right there and waiting to put it back in its case. My dear buddy.

The women were visibly upset that I was stopping, but I gave the girls there a big compliment: I said I couldn't wait to hear more Indigo Girls songs.

I grabbed a beer and drank the entire thing down in a few big gulps. I was thirsty after all that hard work. What I had also done with my performance was solidify that Smokey and I would each be hooking up that weekend. The women were all crowded around us now, talking us both up and offering me compliments on my singing and playing.

Smokey kept looking over at me with that giant smile full of teeth, and I would nod and smile back. She was so happy. The girls were surrounding her, too, and she was bragging about me, telling them I was her best friend.

The other women kept playing around the fire. We walked back to the beach, by the big flames, and stood around laughing with them all. They liked us. We were the "out-of-towners," and the hot commodity. We kept drinking and partying.

At one point, I walked up the path, because I had to piss. Along the way, I met a woman. She grabbed my arm and walked with me. She was talking my ear off the entire way. When we reached the outhouse, I asked her if she had to go. I was going to offer she go first, but she didn't have to. She had been watching me and had followed me to the path. I went in and did my business. When I came out, she had her shirt off and was smiling at me. I walked over to her, because she was standing on the path to return to the beach. She grabbed me and started kissing me.

She was cute, so I was into it. We kissed on that path for a couple of minutes. Then she started dragging me over to the other side of the trees, towards where the cabins and tents were. She brought us over to one of the small tents, unzipped the door, and shoved me inside.

She came in after me and closed the zipper again. She pushed me down on my back and started undoing my pants. I was like, "Whoa, I'm not used to such aggression." But, I also loved it. It was usually me tearing off some straight woman's pants, not me being thrown back and having my pants torn off by another Dyke.

She had short hair and was ultra butch. I wouldn't have thought us compatible, but in this tent, and in this situation, we were most definitely compatible. She started to go down on me, but I was kind of bored. I wanted to be back at the party. I'm sure I groaned and moaned a bit, to get her to be done with it. Just as I was letting out a little yelp of enjoyment, I heard, "Miss Elaineous? Is that you?"

It was Smokey. She had been worried about me, and when I hadn't come back to the fire after going to the washroom, she had started out looking for me. She had heard commotion, and then my voice, and was now standing right outside the tent where I was, pantless, inside. I laughed out loud.

"Yeah, buddy. It's me. I'm coming!"

I pushed the woman off of me.

"That's my best friend," I said. "I'm here with her. I gotta go."

"What?" She was instantly disappointed.

"Hey, thanks," I said as I stumbled bent in half pulling up my pants and crawled out of the tent. Smokey helped me up to my feet.

"I'll see you back at the fire?"

I looked back at her sitting in the doorway of her tent.

"Sorry," I said as Smokey pulled me by the arm back up the trail. I felt slightly bad that I hadn't at least reciprocated the woman's loving of my body, but, hey, I was here to party with my friends. Just because she'd sidelined me en route to the washrooms was not a good enough reason for me to stay back with her.

Smokey and I made our way back to the fire. On the way, I asked if she'd come with me to grab some ingredients to make a big batch of swamp water, a homemade specialty of mine to drink by the fire. She was into it, so we stopped at our cabin.

I had brought the big glass jar and all the ingredients for it with me. Now I put it all in a bag and carried it down to the beach. We got back to the fire, and Miss Carole was there with Trina. I started setting up my big batch of swamp water. I took the lid off the big jar. It was like a giant, 1.9-litre pickle jar. That's what I was using at the time. I had a twenty-sixer of rum, and half of that went in first. Then I added a melted can of frozen orange juice. Splash, in it went. After pulling the tab, I put in a can of crushed pineapple, slopping it into the jar, too. Then I snapped the lid off a jar of maraschino cherries and poured them in. Now the jar was almost full, but I had a can of 7UP to add yet. I looked up at Smokey and Miss Carole, who were both watching me, and turned the can upside down, pouring it into the jar.

Well, didn't the jar totally overflow and all the mix start pouring out onto the beach? I looked at Miss Carole. She was laughing and rolling her eyes at me.

"Did you think?" she said.

Smokey and I dropped to the ground laughing, because, yeah, I had thought, but hadn't cared. That was obvious.

I was drunk and stupid and messy. The contents of the jar were all in layers, not even stirred, because I didn't have anything to stir it with. We tried to swirl the swamp water around by moving it in circles with our hands, but it just kept pouring over the top.

I took a big gulp, trying to empty it down a bit. I almost barfed, it was so strong with rum, and so sweet. We all laughed more. Then Smokey drank from it and passed it around. Miss Carole drank from it—everyone did. Except Trina. It was too beneath her to take part, but she watched all of us as we passed that jar around and my swamp water helped the party level up.

By the end of the night, and by that I mean four in the morning, we were knackered after hours of partying, and the drive, and all of it. It was time to head to the cabin. Most of the other lesbians were gone, and it was down to just the wildest of the partiers now.

Smokey had picked up a woman and brought her back to the cabin. She had her on the bottom bunk with her. I had picked up by the end of the night too, with another gorgeous lesbian, and had her with me on the top bunk. Miss Carole and Tina were on their little bed. We all passed out. At one point, I woke up having to pee. All I could hear were lesbians snoring like black bears scattered around the room. I hopped down from my top bunk and walked out into the damp morning. Everyone else was asleep.

I went to the outhouse in the low light of dawn, then drunkenly made my way back to the cabin and snuggled into my bed with I didn't even know her name.

The next day was a lot like the first night. We partied hard again. The women Smokey and I had hooked up with had gone back to their friends. Which was nice. There were no hard feelings. Everyone was all friendly and happy when they woke up.

The second Smokey got out of bed, she opened the cooler, got us each out a beer, and it was on. We went down to the beach and had a swim and kept drinking all day long in the hot sun.

Unlike the night before, by the time nighttime came that day, we were mumbling, stumbling fools. Not only could I not play the guitar and sing, but I couldn't do anything. I was too drunk. I just propped myself up with my beers and my joints. Thankfully, Smokey was in similar shape, and we just called ourselves Frick and Frack. We sat against a pile of logs and watched all the lesbians partying around us. We were phenomenally drunk and would lean into each other and mumble shit and then giggle.

Miss Carole came over to us multiple times throughout the night to laugh at us. We were so silly. She didn't quite party like we did. She was still trying to impress Trina. But, Miss Carole lived vicariously through both of us that weekend, and told us as much.

I don't even know how we made it back to the cabin at the end of Saturday night, but we did. We didn't pick up that night, though. Every time a lesbian would come over to us and try to chat us up or mention my playing or try to speak with us, we'd lean into each other and laugh. I think most of them were offended, thinking we were laughing at them, but, honestly, we were so drunk that it was all we could do.

The next morning, we were deathly hungover and had a three-plus-hour drive ahead of us. I wasn't looking forward to it in that shape. I had to work on Monday morning, as well. The party was most definitely over. I was sore and grumpy and sick.

Miss Carole was all cheery, though. And Smokey was, too. It never mattered how hungover or sick Smokey was; she was always happy. Me, I was sick. So sick. I've always had the worst hangovers. Or maybe it's just the inhuman amount of alcohol I would drink. Either way, the fun was done.

But damn, did we ever laugh on the way home about how much fun those Sault Ste. Marie girls were.

17

LESBIAN LOVE SHACK

Benny continued to run D-Bar and started having me perform there regularly. I did a couple of solo nights, some of which ended up being quite their own stories (see *Dyke, A Memoir* for the details).

After some time had passed Benny begged me to play with Dawn again for a show, and I did. It was a great show, we played song after song and everyone was totally enthralled by us. She had moved on and was with someone else, and I was far away from her now socially, so it worked out alright.

I also met my next lover, Beth, at that sold-out show with Dawn. Benny was thrilled that we had filled the place. And I found love. All around, it was an excellent night.

Beth and I got hot and heavy pretty fast after meeting and it was only a few months before I moved in with her and her child, Ariel. Beth had a big house in Minnow Lake, and we quickly became a family. It was a far cry from the past few years of partying, but I was ready to settle down and lay low for a bit. And we did lay low, for the first little while.

I taught Beth how to play the guitar and sing, and most evenings we'd hang out at home and play music together. We did like to have lesbians over and party at home, but we didn't go out to the bar as much.

There were also lesbians living across the street—a couple in a downstairs apartment and a couple in an upstairs apartment. In total there were three of us lesbian couples on one short, dead-end street in Sudbury. The other couples had lots of lesbian gatherings at their places, too. So, you won't be surprised to hear that everyone called our street Lesbian Lane.

While I lived with Beth, we would have fire parties. We'd invite the lesbians over to party in our big backyard, around the fire we'd stoke there. We were the last house on the street. Beside and behind us was only rock and woods. We only had one direct neighbour. It was fun to have fires back there, and predictably, the lesbians would show up with their guitars.

Lesbians did love a good house party. Having a house party or going to a house party was, it seemed, almost always favoured over going out to the bar, if there was a choice.

Whereas, the gay boys were historically more interested in the hooking up part, and the bar was a good platform for that. It was often said, and I believe it as well, if it were not for gay men, we would never have had the thriving gay scene we had, all the gay bars of the nineties. Gay women didn't do that. Gay men did that. It was gay men who had all the disposable income from great-paying jobs, usually no children, and often the promiscuity that went along with gay culture.

❧

Beth and I had a couple of beautiful years of being together and lesbian house parties. Then it was all over. I left and got an apartment living above a member of my new ball team. I'd started playing ball again the summer after Beth and I broke up. I was playing on a mixed straight team. The other players were all pretty damn open and positive about me being an openly butch Dyke, and a couple of them became great friends of mine.

That summer was filled with ball parties on weekends and D-Bar at night. D-Bar now had a woman managing it, which wasn't as fun as when Benny had been running it. We were down to one gay bar again in Sudbury, leaving us little options for social gatherings. It didn't matter who was managing it or working the bar; it was our place.

Benny had moved back to Ottawa while I was with Beth. He was now running the biggest gay club in the nation's capital. It sounded like a big deal every time he'd call and fill me in on his new life and latest stories. When he finally got me down there as well, it truly was all that.

Benny called me up one day and told me about his boss, who was this incredible, seasoned piano man. Benny had told his boss all about me, as well, including about my voice, my performing ability, and my skills running a kitchen. Then Benny got me a job there.

It was an exciting opportunity, and it didn't take me much thought or time at all to make the decision to move to Ottawa. I felt like I had been waiting to leave Sudbury my entire life.

When I arrived in Ottawa, I had a suitcase, a guitar case, and three hundred dollars in my pocket. I slept on Benny's couch for two weeks, waiting for his roommate at the time to move out. Then I lived with Benny while I got on my feet in my new, big city. Those were some wild times. From the moment I arrived in Ottawa, it was a party, one that would go on for months for me.

When I settled into my new home in the new big city, I was hoping it would be like Church Street in Toronto, where I had felt so open and alive, and like I had finally found my home. A place where gays didn't have to hide, or get hurt if they weren't hiding, like in

Sudbury. A place where I would be accepted for who I was, and treated with respect for my differences. I had dreams that this would be a life-changer move, and it was.

I started playing music with Brad, Benny's boss, right away. We were like two peas in a pod, and we went together musically like jam and bread.

For the first couple of weeks, I literally just lived my best gay life, learning about my new city, and living in a queer community. I met hundreds of people right away while working at the biggest gay club in Ottawa. I was hanging out with all kinds of different folks every day. It was a whirlwind adventure for me, and one I was not accustomed to. The freedom of being openly gay out in public continued to prove addictive for me.

In those first couple of weeks living in Ottawa, I got to know queer people, the queer community, and all of the queer spaces. I was like the proverbial kid in a candy store. Having come from Sudbury, where, except for one brief period, there had only ever been one gay bar at any given time.

This was a gay community that had been thriving for years before I got here. There were multiple gay bars. Hell, there were bars for gay men, bars for lesbians and Dykes, bars for both, bars for druggies, bars for sex, bars for drag queens, bars for hooking up, and bars for entertainment. It didn't matter what you were into; if you were gay, you had a place to go and enjoy or experience that. That was queer life in the nineties. We had it all.

It was like having a giant community of gays, all over the downtown core of Ottawa. The downtown, which is called Centretown in Ottawa, was where many gay people lived, as well, wanting to be as close to other queer people as possible.

Living downtown and walking along Bank Street and Somerset Street or any of the streets in and around there, you couldn't help but run into swaths of gays. You'd walk past gays in the street.

Gays would be at tables, having breakfast in the restaurants. Gays would fill the coffee shops. And the bars were packed to capacity with gay people every, single night that they were open.

For a Sudbury girl, it was all over-the-top exciting, exhilarating, and eye-opening. After having been beaten up multiple times in Sudbury just for being gay, it was like a dream come true. This was so much more than just refreshing; it felt safe.

It was 1997 when I moved to Ottawa. What a time to be gay. What a time to be in Ottawa. And what a time to have experienced. Let me try to describe what it was like to move to O-town in the heyday of queerness in Canada, at least through the eyes of this ol', Sudbury, butch Dyke.

18

NOT YOUR SUDBURY SATURDAY NIGHT

The day I arrived in Ottawa was a thrilling day for me, and that night it only got better, because Benny had lined up Jeff who worked for him at Icon to give me a tour of the city.

It was a hectic first night and Jeff took me to most of the gay men's hangouts, like Market Station, the Eagle's Nest, and Icon. We partied hard and ended up back at Benny's bar, upstairs at Icon, by the end of the night to finish things off.

During our adventures, Jeff had also brought me down to Zena's, the Dyke bar in the basement of Icon, and I was immediately hooked. I needed to go back and really experience the Dyke bar, not just make a twenty-minute visit like we did together on that first night. I had met the bar manager of Zena's, a cute, real sweet Dyke. I wanted to go back and see her again, too.

Miss Carole was coming to Ottawa to visit. I'd only been in the city a week, but she was coming. She stayed with me at Benny's and we snuggled on the sectional couch all weekend, and partied hard in between. I wanted to show Miss Carole the Dyke bar, as well as Icon, where Benny worked and where I had started training in the kitchen my first week. I was off all weekend and wanted to take in the city properly, but with my dear friend Miss Carole. I knew she'd be as wowed by everything as I had been. And she was.

When she showed up Saturday morning, I was so excited. I hadn't seen her in two weeks, and I felt like my life had changed hugely in only the short time I'd been in the big city. Walking around and being in a queer community was life-altering. I would get up and stroll down Bank Street and around Somerset, do a loop down around O'Connor and back to Catherine, where Benny's apartment was. I'd say hi to everyone and stop to talk to anyone.

It was the opposite of Sudbury in every way. First of all, in Sudbury no one walks, period. There is nowhere to walk to, or it's not part of the culture. The downtown core of Sudbury had lost its flare years before I grew into an adult. In the 90s, it was a broken downtown, full of broken people. The city sprawled so far and wide that everyone needed a car to get around. In Sudbury, you also only knew the people you knew. There weren't many opportunities to meet strangers, not like this.

In Ottawa, I was meeting people left and right, and not just at night at the bars. I was making friends everywhere I went. The coffee shop had queers working at it, the diner as well, and the pharmacy. Everywhere I went there seemed to be a queer person. It was thrilling. They all knew I had started working at Icon, and I was welcomed into the community with open arms. I felt so lucky.

In Sudbury, most of the gay people, in my experience, were only out at night, and then only when they were safely in the only gay bar. Even there, you weren't truly safe, because straight men would bust in and beat up the queers at least once a year. It wasn't safe for queers in Sudbury. It was, and by all means still is, a very homophobic place. I visit at least once a year, and I'm still looked at like I'm an alien when I'm there. Residents there aren't used to openly out, visibly butch Dykes. So, needless to say, Ottawa was dreamy for me.

~

We started drinking pretty much the second Miss Carole arrived. Even Benny, although he had to work that night, had a few beers with us while we smoked joints and caught up with her. Benny and I were still flying on the high of the excitement surrounding my arrival and all of the ways my life was taking shape in Ottawa.

I had met my new piano player and music partner, Brad. We'd hit it off and had already been practicing, getting ready for our first big show together in a few weeks. Miss Carole was super supportive about it, and promised to get that Thursday night off to drive down to Ottawa and join us for my first major performance.

Benny left the apartment at around seven, so he could go open up his bar upstairs at Icon and get ready for the huge Saturday night crowd. I had learned the previous Saturday night, my first night out in the city, that Benny's bar was wall-to-wall gay guys and at capacity on Saturdays.

Benny was the manager and star of the bar, and the men flocked to his space. I had spent most of my late night there the previous Saturday. Now that Miss Carole was in town, I wanted to have a lesbian night with her. We made a plan and told Benny we'd end our night off at his bar with him, but that we were going touring first. I couldn't wait to show Miss Carole around.

We left Benny's apartment on foot and walked up Bank Street. I wanted to show Miss Carole the route I walked each day to get to CP, the bar where I practiced with Brad, and then how I'd bop over to Icon from there. I also showed her my favourite diner, which I was eating at daily, and the gay shops along the street. We didn't cook much at Benny's apartment. I waved through the window at the diner staff inside. In the apartment, we were all night owls, working at night, mostly, and we all ate out, except for home-fried potatoes, which were Benny's go-to. He loved making French fries.

We stopped at CP and had a drink on the patio with some of the boys who recognized me right away now. I'd been there almost every day with Brad the past week, getting to know the place, and the regulars and staff. The boys were all incredibly sweet to us both, buying us drinks and telling stories. Miss Carole's eyes were like saucers whenever she looked over at me.

Then one of the waiters came over and slipped me a little baggie and said to have a great night on him. Although I loved and trusted Miss Carole, and she was one of my best friends, I hid it from her. I didn't want her to know I indulged in hard drugs. She didn't know that about me, and I feared she wouldn't understand or love me as much if she did. I didn't do them regularly, but I certainly did them on occasion, depending on who I was with.

In Sudbury, I'd had friends who dated bikers, and who'd also worked for the bikers, so harder drugs were not taboo for me. Miss Carole, on the other hand, was a good girl. I would never imagine doing cocaine or anything like that with her, so I didn't share those details. I slipped downstairs to the women's washroom and waited for the two gay guys to come out of the stall, where they were doing the exact same thing I was headed in to do. I'm not sure why, but the men always did their lines in the women's washrooms in Ottawa. It was so common, I got used to it, but it did take me aback at first.

I headed back up to the main floor of CP to find Miss Carole in a great conversation with this older Dyke who had come in and started chatting her up. She told us about other Dyke bars in town, info we were quite intrigued about. She told us that the Eagle's Nest had a ladies night on Fridays, with a female Dyke DJ. She also told us about the Coral Reef, the biggest and longest-running Dyke bar in the city. We promised ourselves we'd go there later.

It was dark out and CP was filling up with men, as usual. It was the oldest gay men's bar in Ottawa, with history dating far back. On this particular night, like on many others I would experience,

Bruce House, an organization that offers "Hope, Housing and Support" to those living with HIV and AIDS, was set up at the main entrance of CP, collecting donations and handing out free condoms. I'd see many similar organizations set up at the entrance of CP or at the bottom of the stairs up to Cell Block in the coming years. The AIDS Committee of Ottawa was often there, or the Ottawa Knights, a leather men's group. I'm pretty sure Cell Block the upstairs men's leather bar at CP was taken over once a month by the Ottawa Knights to raise money for charity as well.

Miss Carole and I decided it was time to head over to Zena's at Icon. We downed our beers and said goodbye to all the gay boys who had been so nice and welcoming to us both. We headed out down the front steps of CP and up Somerset to Bank. We crossed at the intersection and started up the couple of blocks to Lisgar Street making our way to Icon. On the way, we passed so many queers. Miss Carole kept glancing at me, and I'd say, "Yep!"

She was pointing with her eyes at every gay person we saw.

"Them? They're gay too?"

It was shocking for us, coming from Sudbury, experiencing this new world where gay people were out on the street.

We were primed and laughing our asses off when we got to the door at Icon. Of course, there was a lineup. I'm pretty good at using my words to get what I want, so I went up the line and spoke with the doorman, who didn't know me. I said I was Benny's best friend from Sudbury and it was like he parted the Red Sea. Spreading his arms out across the lineup, he looked at me, and said, "Come through."

"Um, my friend is back there in line," I said. "Can I get her too?"

"Yes, make it quick."

I yelled my bloody head off for Miss Carole to come meet me at the door, she ran up, and we bolted inside. We stopped at the coat check, not to give our coats, since we weren't wearing any, but to give the guy there two bucks. Benny had mentioned to me it was always good to give the coat check people two dollars, even if you didn't have a coat. He explained that they were the eyes and ears of the place, and if you wanted information, or if you needed to know anything, you could go to them if you were a regular tipper. I learned the ins and outs like that quickly living with Benny.

Miss Carole and I said hi to the coat check boy and tossed him a two-dollar bill. He winked at us both.

"Thanks, ladies!" he said. That was code; he had our backs.

I was eager to get Miss Carole into the basement to Zena's. I damn well knew she had never been to a Dyke bar, either, but I also wanted to give her the royal tour, so I did that first. We started on the main floor and said hi to Freddy and Jason, the main floor bartender and waiter, who were already serving a hopping section in their space.

We stood at the bar and drank a beer with Jason. He was a short, cute, little, boisterous gay boy. His server Freddy was my darling from the second I had met him last weekend on my first visit. He was amazingly generous and loving and full of energy.

"Let's go," I said after our drink.

I grabbed Miss Carole by the waist, pulling her towards the door, where the stairs led down to the Dyke bar. There was a lineup to get in there, as well, but again I used my charm and this time mentioned knowing Genevieve, the Dyke bar manager at Zena's, whom I'd met last weekend. They let us through.

I also told them I was from Sudbury. That seemed to get you anywhere in those days, because Benny was from Sudbury. He managed the entire building for the owners, my music partner, Brad, and his partner Donald.

Genevieve was from Sudbury, one of Benny's servers upstairs was from Sudbury, and the guy I was taking over for at Icon was also from Sudbury. Funny enough, in Ottawa, saying you were from "Sudbury" was well received back then, the opposite of what I would have thought coming from what felt like such a dark, shitty place. But, that word and city had some clout, which I found both funny and exciting. To think saying that you're from Sudbury would get anyone anything was a joke to me, but it worked here. We were the outsiders, the new people, the wildlings from "the north." We could party and drink hard and work, and do all three at the same time. We were primed and already such mega-alcoholics that we ran circles around the Ottawa gang. We were just more used to all the drinking.

In Sudbury, gay people drank a lot. Well, everyone in Sudbury drank a lot, but especially the gays. They did drugs, too, but it was harder to get the stronger drugs in Sudbury, and I think those were more available in straight bars and the biker bars at the time. Cocaine wasn't available at the gay bar in Sudbury until D Bar because it was owned by the same owners that owned a straight biker bar down the street. That was when the coke showed up in the gay community in Sudbury.

When you live in such a homophobic place, city, and dark environment, it kind of makes sense to drink a lot. But also, drinking was very socially condoned at the time. In many ways, I also think that some of us got drunk to survive our queerness. When we grew up and became adults, and only had straight places where people were wildly homophobic to hang out in, we got messed up to deal with it which then, in turn, made us unwittingly complicit. The loneliness of being the only queer, most often in the closet and hiding, made for a hard life.

Then, when we did find the gay bar, we'd get completely drunk there too. Everything we were doing was the opposite of what we had been taught and told we should be doing in the world. We all had this self-loathing attitude and shame. We always felt like we were hiding. Gay bars mostly being hidden away in basements played into that feeling, as well. If you were gay, it was much easier to be the outsider, to cover up, hide out, be yourself, and be sexual, if you were drunk or drinking. Also, there wasn't any real culture in Sudbury, like arts or theatre or a music industry to speak of. Everyone grew up using alcohol as entertainment. It was extremely normalized.

I started drinking at ten years old, when I was made by my parents to bartend all their parties. They didn't force me; that's not what I mean. But, they put me there and taught me to do it. I loved doing it, and learned to make money at it, which was cool. But then, I started making a drink or two for the people at the partiers, and I'd pour myself one, too. It was the way it was, kind of like drinking and driving; everyone had always done it in Sudbury.

When Miss Carole and I walked up to the bar at Zena's, Genevieve recognized me right away. She came over to us and greeted me enthusiastically.

"Hey, Sudbury Dyke! You're back."

"Yeah. And I brought another Sudbury Dyke with me. Miss Carole meet Genevieve. She's the big Dyke in charge down here."

Miss Carole gushed, as did I. Genevieve was hot and sweet and in control. Watching her was thrilling.

Miss Carole started tugging on my shirt. I was busy looking at the hundreds of Dykes in the bar, eyeing it all. They were at every table in swaths. They were standing everywhere. The bar was surrounded with Dykes ordering drinks. The dance floor was so packed you couldn't tell where it started and ended. Miss Carole was still tugging on me.

"I know, I know. Isn't it marvelous?" I said.

"No! Miss Elaineous. Fuck, look," she said. She turned my head with her fingers until I was facing the back of the bar. And I saw him. He was there, as if I were watching a television. Like I was watching him sitting on the side stage, awaiting his score after a triple Salchow. There was an imaginary spotlight on his beautiful face, and he was smiling. Then he saw me, seeing him. He was so beautiful. I was dying.

"Holy shit," I thought. "I knew it. I knew we'd see famous people here."

Genevieve went over. She was speaking with him.

"Holy fuck!" I said.

"See, I'm freaking out," Miss Carole answered.

"Oh my god, Miss Carole. It's fucking Brian Orser!"

You might think we'd seen k.d. lang or some other famous lesbian, since we were in a Dyke bar, but no. No, it wasn't a woman at all. It was a man, and a very famous man. It was Olympian, Canadian national champion and world champion figure skater Brian Orser. He was shoulder-to-shoulder with another sweet, handsome boy, and they were talking it up with Genevieve.

We were fully star struck. Now was when you could tell we were from Sudbury and never saw famous people. We had to go over. So, we did. Miss Carole and I made our way over to the rear middle of the bar, where they were seated. I was wondering why they weren't being surrounded by all the Dykes. When we got to them, they both looked at us and smiled. I guess they could see the fire in our wide eyes as we approached them with these huge "Oh my god. You're *Brian Orser*" smiles on our faces.

"Um, we just want to say hi and tell you that we love you," I said, "and we're from Sudbury and we're so proud of you and ...."

It makes me laugh so hard right now, thinking of this story. We went on and on, both of us. We were both big figure skating fans. I used to be *in love* with Michelle Kwan, another champion figure skater, but American. I think everyone in Sudbury watched figure skating. I know my parents did, and my grandparents. We'd always watch the championships. Maybe it was because it was what was on television and we only had two channels back then, but we always watched it.

Brian smiled his giant, gorgeous smile.

"Thank you," he said softly. He was seriously that sweet.

That was it. His boyfriend said thanks and shook our hands. We left him there and we scuttled away, all giggly. It was exciting. It was Miss Carole's first night in Ottawa and we had already seen someone famous. She was elated. I was, too.

We spent the rest of the night dancing and meeting tons of people. We were here, we were there. One second, we were on the dance floor together, the next second I saw her across the room chatting up a group of Dykes, then she was at the back, playing pool. We worked the room. There were so many women in that space, it was like the Dinah Shore weekend in there.

By the end of the night, I was wrapped in a stage curtain on the dance floor. But, I had the curtain wrapped around myself and another Dyke and we were kissing inside it. I was wild and happy to be with Miss Carole. She was making out with another chick at a table in the corner. Genevieve had taken extra good care of us all night. We didn't pay for a thing. That was Genevieve. The drinks kept coming, in fact, probably because we were from Sudbury and Genevieve adored us for that reason alone.

Miss Carole and I had so much fun. We were like kids who had never been out before, wild and crazy, and meeting and talking to everyone. It was almost too much fun to handle.

19
______

ORAL GRIEF

I continued to work in the kitchen at Icon while Brad and I rehearsed for our big show at CP's Silhouette Lounge. We had been practicing for two weeks and our big night was this Thursday. It would be my first performance with Brad in the little piano lounge.

Miss Carole was coming up from Sudbury and bringing a couple of girls with her, and Benny took the night off. Some new friends and staff mates from both Icon and CP were all planning on coming too. I was pumped and ready. Brad and I had been working intensively, and had a full set ready to go. Mostly Fleetwood Mac songs from the *Rumours* album, a bunch of Melissa Etheridge and k.d. lang songs, and Brad sang a bunch of Elton John. I was singing some beautiful harmony on his numbers. We felt good about what we had pulled together in only a couple of weeks. It was all so smooth and perfect; it was a joyous musical partnership, right from the very start, for Brad and me.

The big night did not disappoint. We packed the place and Brad and I wowed everyone. Our little piano lounge was so full that people spilled out into the hallway by the downstairs washrooms.

I made lots of tips that night, and Brad was ecstatic at the momentum and sheer size of the crowd that we drew. He kept looking at me all night, grinning and with smiley eyes. He was immensely proud.

It made me proud, too. To do this, for us to be successful at it, and for them to all have loved us. It was magical. The crowd cheered all night, and was extremely pleased with our performance.

After the show, Miss Carole and a gang from the bar came back to our place. I was still living at Benny's, but I had my own room now in the basement, next to Benny and Chad, his partner at the time. We talked about our night and everyone toasted me and Brad. Miss Carole was also incredibly proud, as was Benny. They were beaming. Benny had brought me here and Miss Carole had followed me here. We were all living our best lives.

By the wee morning, we had all retired to our rooms. There were women staying over upstairs. All over the living room, people were crashed out. Miss Carole came downstairs to sleep in my bed. We slept in quite late the next day.

When we awoke, we heard everyone upstairs already awake, and the party was back on. We could hear Benny telling stories, with his big, belting voice and laughter. Miss Carole and I, still lying in bed, looked at each other and laughed, sharing in a moment to ourselves.

"I'm so proud of you," she said.

"Aww, thanks, sweetie. I'm so happy you could come for my show. And now we get to spend the entire weekend together."

I had the weekend off. Brad and I wouldn't start playing all weekend down in the piano lounge for a couple of weeks yet. I only worked the kitchen at Icon during weeknights. I had all weekend to show Miss Carole around.

The other girls from Sudbury had to go back for a ball tournament, so they were leaving. As soon as they got up, they had a quick bite to eat and a few laughs, then headed back to Sudbury.

Miss Carole was staying the weekend with me, though, and tonight we were going to the Eagle's Nest. Then we were headed to the famous lesbian bar we had heard about, the Coral Reef. The Dyke we'd met who had described it to us called it the Oral Grief, which made us both laugh. That's what I continued to call it, we all did.

That night when we got to Ottawa's Byward Market in our taxi, Miss Carole was enthused. I had made it special. I had the cabby take us all the way past Parliament Hill, so Miss Carole could be as thrilled as I was when I first arrived and drove by it. She didn't disappoint, putting her window down and taking in the massive structure and iconic view.

"Isn't it something?" she said. "Like being right there on the stamp."

Miss Carole looked at me with tears in her eyes. She was emotional. I placed my hand on her leg as we continued into the Market and onto York Street. I had the taxi let us out right at the corner by all the market stalls, so Miss Carole could see them. It was fall and getting late for vendors, but there were still lots of people around and it was all so exhilarating for us.

When we got to the Eagle's Nest, there was a lineup down the street to the door. But, it was all women in line, so we didn't mind. We right away started chatting the women up and meeting as many as we could. I am extremely outgoing and will speak to anyone. And Miss Carole? Same, same. She would talk to anyone. Plus, we were friggin' joyous. We beamed at anyone who looked at us, telling everyone who would listen that we were from Sudbury.

We found right away that women here were kind of taken with us. I think we were more confident and outgoing than most of them.

We were like a party duo unleashed on the Ottawa lesbians. We wanted to literally talk to every woman in the lineup. And we did our best.

In the bar, it was lady's night, and it was packed. We couldn't get out to the balcony, so I couldn't show Miss Carole the view of the Market and how it looked from up there. That was what I had been planning to do with her, so I was a bit disappointed. It was too crowded, and the music was too loud for us to talk to anyone, or even ourselves.

We made our way to the bar. It took twenty minutes to get a drink, and then we paid nearly seven bucks a beer each. That set our moods back a notch. Hell, you could still get a beer in Sudbury for three bucks. We instantly weren't pleased. It felt off, the two of us shoulder-to-shoulder, watching a room full of rowdy women, and not being one of them. We were bored, so we decided to head over to the Coral Reef. But, we did finish our drinks first.

We stood against the wall near the bar, drank our drinks that we had waited far too long to for, and women-watched for a bit. That was fun, because they were all young and hot. Miss Carole and I smiled at each other a lot. We didn't stay, though. We both wanted a different scene.

We started down the stairs and passed some women I had met the week before at Icon. We told them we were headed over to the Coral Reef, and they said they'd be over there later. We smiled. That was nice. We hadn't talked to anyone since we were in the lineup earlier, which had ended up being the most fun we had at the Eagle's Nest that night.

As we walked through the famous Ottawa Market, Miss Carole remarked on all the beautiful things she was seeing. The buildings were much older than anything Sudbury had to offer, and the structure of the Market itself was something of a novelty to us.

When we got to the Rideau Centre, we didn't know where to go, so we looked around for the parking garage where the Coral Reef was supposed to be. We walked around the building and asked a few people. They pointed us down a side street, so we headed that way. The area was starting to feel a bit dodgy, like Sudbury. But that was fine for us; nothing new there. Dark street, dark lane, parking garage, bar in the basement. Yeah, this felt very familiar to both of us.

When we got to the parking garage entrance, we didn't see anything. There was nothing but cars going in and out of an underground garage. We were confused, but then our luck changed. We saw three raging Dykes—I mean, spiked hair, no hair, and orange hair, going in through a grey door at the side of the parking garage.

"There," I said, pointing to the three different women heading inside.

"Yes," Miss Carole nodded.

We skipped across the driveway entrance to the garage, then over to the other side where the unmarked door was, and where we had seen the three women disappear. I looked at Miss Carole, she looked at me, and we dove into that blacked-out door. It slammed behind us. As we walked inside, we were in a dark hallway with posters covering every inch of the walls. We got to the end of the hallway, and there was a Dyke behind glass. She asked for our ID. She made us sign our names on a list. We said we were from Sudbury and she rolled her eyes at us. She didn't care.

"Sign in, please," she grumbled.

We did and then we followed the music into the space. When we got there, we stood, not speaking, not moving, just looking. We were in awe, looking all around us at what felt like a movie set from an old Dyke western. There were women in cowboy hats, and some in full suits. There were women dancing, and a hot Dyke up in the DJ booth, who waved down at us as we looked up at her, gushing.

"Oh, she's hot," Miss Carole blurted out.

"Yep. Sure is," I said.

We walked over to the bar. I got us each a beer and a shot of tequila. We downed our shots and guzzled our beers behind them, then we each ordered another. There was no waiting for a drink here. This beer was to walk around the place with. We decided to go stand next to the DJ booth and watch everything unfold from there.

It really was like being on a movie set. Unlike at Zena's, we didn't just jump in there and party. It wasn't like that in here. It was different. First of all, the women were all a lot older than they were at Zena's, and it was very evident this was a community of its own. The women here were grey-haired, and wore suits, and all seemed to know each other. They were super masculine. We thought it was funny, although we knew ol' gals back home who dressed that way, too. Yeah, we thought they were funny; not in a laughing at them kind of way, but in a holy shit, these are our elders kind of way. This would be us one day. Also, these were the Dykes who had forged the way for us. These were our heroes, and we were in awe of them all. We'd both never seen so many older Dykes before. It seems most of the lesbians we knew back home were our age, or just a bit older.

We stood, holding our beers, watching everyone. But, I think we watched the DJ the most. She jumped down from her perch and an older DJ went up to continue spinning. The younger DJ came over to us with a big smile, and we both became stiff and shy. It was weird. I'd never seen either of us shut up like that before. We were both smitten with her.

She could tell and she loved it. We were tripping over our words, but we told her our names. She introduced herself as DJ Tim, and we liked that. We smiled and both shook her hand and offered to buy her a beer, and she liked that. Miss Carole took off to the bar to get that beer for her, working hard to impress her, while I stayed behind and kept chatting with DJ Tim.

When Miss Carole came back, me and DJ Tim were heavy into a conversation, face-to-face. We had hit it off immediately. Miss Carole going to the bar gave DJ Tim an opportunity to ask me if I was into the fun stuff.

"Hell, yeah," I said. I explained I was definitely into the fun stuff, but that my friend wasn't.

"Great. Then we better hurry," she said.

She grabbed my hand and pulled me over to a door near the entrance, then pushed us both in through it. It was the washroom, and she shoved me into one of the stalls. She turned me around and kissed me.

"Holy shit." I pulled back from her kiss. "I thought we were coming in here to do a line of coke."

"We are, silly," she said.

She turned and pulled a little paper envelope out of her tight jean pocket and unfolded it, then dabbed a line for both of us. She pulled a bill out of her other pocket, rolled it up like a pro, and passed it over to me.

"Guests first." She smiled.

I bent over and snorted the line, then passed the rolled bill back to her and she did the same. Then she stood up, came at me, and kissed me again. That was when Miss Carole came into the washroom and yelled, "Miss Elaineous?"

I pulled away.

"Yeah. Yeah, I'm here, babe."

DJ Tim and I came out of the stall. I knew I had to hide doing the coke from Miss Carole. Well, I didn't have to, but I did. It was kind of the way coke was at the time. If you did it, you knew who else did it. Or it would be easy to figure it out. It always was. If you did it, you know what I'm talking about. If you didn't, especially never like my Miss Carole, it was the last thing on earth you'd suspect anyone doing. That was the case here. I grabbed the DJ and kissed her again. As we walked out of the stall, I looked at Miss Carole.

"Just smooching with the DJ, buddy," I said, and we all laughed as we grabbed our beers from Miss Carole. Then we headed back out into the crowded room.

DJ Tim was now with us, and, more specifically, with me. Miss Carole was happy and started moving through the crowd of Dykes looking to hook up herself.

We spent the night partying at the Oral Grief, the DJ and I, in and out of the bathroom all night. Of course, Miss Carole thought we kept going in there to make out. Each time she'd see us come out, she'd look at us and grin and wink, and we would do the same back at her. I didn't like lying to Miss Carole, or leaving out that detail. But, I also knew how to keep my pieces in their places. There was no harm in not telling her. So, I didn't.

When the place started winding down, we decided to hop in a cab to get back to Benny's. DJ Tim was coming, and Miss Carole had teamed up with a sweet and fun woman named Sheyanne, who was coming home with us, too.

Miss Carole ended up making out on the big sectional couch upstairs at Benny's with her new friend for the rest of the night. I took the DJ down to my room and we humped for what seemed like hours in our blurry, coked-out daze.

I woke up Sunday having to say goodbye to my dear friend Miss Carole, again. I hated when she had to leave. It made me homesick, not for Sudbury, just for her. She promised she'd be back, but

I knew she had a big run up north with CN coming up and I wouldn't be seeing her for at least another month. It was hard to say goodbye, especially after the big weekend we had experienced together.

Miss Carole would come back, but things would be a bit different on her next visit.

20

FRANKY'S ON FRANK

During my first two months living in Ottawa, I worked in the kitchen at Icon every Sunday brunch then Monday through Thursday during the week, then Brad and I had our "ladies night" show at CP on Thursday nights, and I had my weekends off. That proved to not be the best for me, a wild, butch Dyke who'd just arrived in the big city. I had far too much time on my hands.

After living at Benny's for two months, I decided I needed to move out to maintain our good relationship. I loved Benny tremendously. That he'd gotten me to Ottawa, and the fact of our lifelong friendship, it all meant so much to me. But, he and Chad were arguing a lot. It was triggering for me, and it was making me resent them both. I had to leave. It was just normal relationship fighting, but I didn't feel like being around it anymore. The guys kept long, hard hours at the bar, and would get home late, talk loudly or argue, and I'd always be woken up. I didn't like living there anymore. I also thought maybe I needed to live with some Dykes.

DJ Tim from the Oral Grief and I kept hanging out together. We never dated, but we'd get messed up and then we'd fool around a bit. We were like good friends with benefits, all casual, like the gay dudes did it. Working at CP and Icon, both owned, run and completely staffed by gay men, I was surrounded by gay male culture, and I guess it rubbed off on me.

DJ Tim brought me to a new bar I hadn't been to yet, one that no one at Icon or CP had mentioned to me, called Franky's on Frank. It was a big, three-storey, brownstone house turned into a three-level gay bar, similar to CP. The front of the brownstone had big pillars surrounding a front porch, with steps to go up into the building. Each pillar had the different colours of the gay rainbow, an obvious nod to the queer community.

In those days, seeing a rainbow flag, door sticker, sign, or any kind of rainbow was a symbol of safety, openness, and positivity. It was a symbol that made me feel instantly at ease and comfortable, safe, and invited. I always went into shops that displayed the rainbow flag in one way or another, and, most every time, it was owned either by a gay person or someone very gay-positive. "Friends of Dorothy" was another term we used back then to say they were people who liked the gays. Dorothy being Dorothy from *The Wizard of Oz*, as she and Judy Garland, the woman who played the character in the movie, were forever gay icons. If anyone ever told you that someone was a friend of Dorothy, or that a shop was a friend of Dorothy, that meant they were gay-positive, and you could go there, or shop there without fear.

The top floor at Franky's had male strip shows and drag shows. It was dark and campy, with a lot of low, comfy furniture, a dim, curtained-off stage area against one wall, and a blacked-out window. The second floor had a pub-like feel, with a couple of bars at different ends, and a pool table in a room at the back.

The basement? Well, I never went down there.

I had heard Franky's used to be called Chez Nous, but the owner had changed it. I think I liked Chez Nous better, but Franky's on Frank was easy to remember. It was such a cool spot. In Sudbury, we didn't have bars like this, these old houses converted into bars. I thought it was fantastic.

When I was at Franky's with DJ Tim, I met this sweet, little gay man, Tommy Boy. He was tiny and blond and hella cute, and all the boys wanted him and he knew it. He was from Newfoundland and had the sweetest accent, I've always had a thing for Newfoundland accents. We hit it off. He worked at a diner on Elgin Street during the day, and at Franky's at night.

He introduced me to "The Purse." Her real name was Kathy, but everyone called her The Purse. She was a coke dealer. I had seen her at CP a couple of times. She'd run in with her big purse and head downstairs. Then we'd see her run out of the place. She never stayed or stood around; she ran in and ran out.

"People to see," she'd say.

I think it was partially her not wanting to stay in one place, so as to not get caught dealing. But, also, The Purse liked her product a little too much. She was high as a kite all the time. If you know what it's like to be on that drug, then you'll know it comes with a lot of fast, erratic movements and actions. That was The Purse in a nutshell.

She was good friends with Tommy Boy. I thought they went way back or something, because they acted like they were good, old friends, but I'd later learn that it was The Purse who was supplying Tommy Boy with coke to sell. It was another thing I found out he was doing at Franky's, and probably at the diner on Elgin, as well. The Purse was his connection, and he'd sell for her. She was always checking in, restocking and taking her cut. Like I said, it wasn't all obvious to me at first, but it never takes me too long to figure this shit out.

DJ Tim and I hung out at Franky's a lot. It was only two streets from where Benny lived. We'd walk over and be there until they closed the place. One day, she told me that there was this great house on the corner of Kent and Gladstone, only a few blocks away, that was for rent. She said it had four big bedrooms and was huge. I could see her side-eyeing me as she told me this. She was testing whether I'd be interested. I don't think she thought I would be, but she didn't know what was going on at home, and my discomfort with it all. She was surprised when I jumped all over it.

"Have you seen it? How much is the rent? Is it nice?" I was asking every question in the book. She had no answers for me, so we decided she'd get the number off the house on her way back home. Then she'd call to get us an appointment to look at it. I thought that was great. It filled me with anticipation. I wanted to move on and get another place. I loved my Benny and I wasn't going to let him and his shitty relationship ruin our lifelong friendship. This was their thing and I needed to let it be. It was hard, though, because I wanted to jump in there all the time and try to help them.

DJ Tim got us an appointment to see the place on Kent, and we went and looked it over. We liked it right away. It was old and had lots of character, more than I'd ever had in a place I lived. It had brick interior walls and was enormous. The bedrooms upstairs had twelve-foot ceilings and were very large, and each main room on the first floor was massive. When the management company rep told us it was twelve hundred dollars a month, and we'd need first and last, DJ Tim and I looked at each other. We nodded, said we'd call them back soon, and left.

We needed to find a couple of roommates to make this happen. We couldn't do it on our own with our part-time jobs. I was only making minimum wage in the kitchen at Icon. With only one night at CP at the time singing, I didn't make that much money. DJ Tim was barely working, just DJ'ing on weekends.

She had this friend, Sharon, who worked for the government. DJ Tim told me about her needing a place.

"Yes," I said.

Then we went to the diner on Elgin to have breakfast. We saw Tommy Boy there and told him about our new place. He said he wanted in, since he was looking for a new pad as well.

In one day, we got it all figured out. DJ Tim called her friend Sharon, who jumped at the opportunity. She loved the location and could walk to work downtown to her government building each day. We called the rental company back and said we'd take it and move in on the first, which was only one week away. It all happened very fast. We gathered all our money to pay first and last month, and we did it.

I told Benny I was moving. He found someone to move into my room right away. At that time, it wasn't hard to find roommates. We all worked in gay bars, and queers were always looking for places downtown, so it was smooth and easy. Benny wasn't mad at all that I was moving out; he was totally supportive. In fact, he was excited for me and couldn't wait to come check out my new place, so that pleased me. The last thing I wanted was to upset him.

My ball team from Sudbury had brought all my furniture down to Ottawa when they visited to party with me in the big city, from the little apartment I'd had right before I left there. They had put it in a U-Haul truck, so I had most of the furniture we'd need for our new place. I had a big, retro dining room table with chairs, a big couch, a coffee table, dishes, cutlery. I had all the major stuff.

When we all moved in, it was awesome. I ran upstairs and took the biggest bedroom for myself. DJ Tim took the room at the opposite end of the hall, near the washroom. Her friend Sharon took the bedroom beside her. And right beside me was Tommy Boy. He was a darling and I grew to love him dearly. I still think of him. He's one of only very few people I've lost touch with over the years. I heard that he'd moved back to Newfoundland. It would make sense.

This house was a party hole from day one. We had the biggest bash the night we moved in, and we all went down to Icon afterwards. It was Sunday and we partied there all night with Benny and a bunch of queens in the basement. On Sundays the Dyke bar in the basement at Zena's turned into a drag queen cabaret.

I had worked the brunch shift earlier that morning, and had been at home setting up and drinking all afternoon since. We were toasting our new place, and DJ Tim and Tommy Boy and I were doing lines all day. DJ Tim and Tommy Boy were both selling at this point, so it surrounded me and I never had to pay for it. I'd buy them a beer and they'd give me a line. That was the way it all went.

We partied hard that first night. We were all so pumped about our new place. When the party at Icon was over we invited the entire place, or anyone who was left there at three a.m., to come over and continue the party at our new row-house.

Genevieve the bar manager and a couple of other staff and bus boys came, as did some regulars who were still at the bar at closing. We brought everyone home. The party went until the next day, then continued. We all partied through Monday. Most people stayed. Even Genevieve stayed over that night and slept in my bed. I put her up there in the wee morning when I could see her yawning. She looked so exhausted. We were all on cocaine and partying, and she had been working all night. So, I brought her to my room and she crashed, while we all told stories way too loudly for hours downstairs.

The house party continued until it was time to head out to the bar again. This time, we headed to Franky's. It was Tuesday and they had a deal for two-dollar Tuesdays. The Purse had come by our new place in the middle of the day to drop off more drugs to Tommy Boy. She looked around and said she loved the place. She was nodding and nodding as she walked around and approved of everything, all erratic like she usually was.

She was a funny character. I always liked her. She was weird and confident and tough as nails. The woman was a coke dealer and would go in and out of every bar in the Ottawa downtown core each night. A single woman, by herself, and that was what she did. She sold to the gays, then went in and out of the Duke of Somerset, a straight kind of roughneck bar, and dealt to all the straight people there. If you stood at the corner of Somerset and Bank on any given night, you could see The Purse hopping in and out and around all night long.

She was tough. But, when you looked at her, you didn't see tough. She had longish, red hair, and green eyes, and was very pleasant to look at. More than anything, what made her tough was her attitude. Holy shit, that girl could scare you with a look. Thankfully, she liked me. She'd come into my ladies night at CP's piano lounge and always request this song I covered, called *Space in My Heart*, by the lesbian duo Open Mind. The lyrics that she connected with were "You left a space a mile wide in my heart." The Purse would stand there and nod her head and smile at me when I sang it for her. Then she'd walk up to my tip jar and pop a baggie of cocaine into it, in front of everyone. That sort of thing happened.

We went to Franky's and closed the place up that night, too. We hung out on all three levels throughout the night. DJ Tim and I were playing pool in the back. At one point, when Tommy Boy came in he found us on the pool table. We had our clothes on, but we were doing our humpback jive.

When Franky's closed, we brought everyone back to our place again. It would turn out to be a new nightly routine: party until close, bring the gang back to our house, stay up all night partying and then repeat.

This night, though, I must have made my way to my bedroom at some point and passed out, because, when I woke up at around noon on Wednesday, there was someone in my bed with me. It totally freaked me out at first when I felt a body behind me in bed.

As I was waking up, trying to come up to the light of day in my mind, I got nervous and worried. Then I calmed, thinking it must just be DJ Tim.

You'll be as shocked as I was when I turned over to find a still-in-full-make-up drag queen passed out, naked, in bed with me. It was Maj. I had met her at Franky's last night on one of our trips upstairs for a drag show. I remembered doing lines with her and having fun, but the rest was gone. I did not know how she got in my bed. I looked under the sheets. I had shorts and a T-shirt on, so that made me happy. Not that I would have had a problem, necessarily, with having had sex with a drag queen. But I'm a Dyke, so that wasn't where I was at.

When she started to open her eyes, I was staring right at her, leaning over her face, still trying to figure it all out. Her eyes popped open and she screamed in my face. I jumped. We both laughed.

Tommy Boy came running in, giggling. He ran to the end of my bed, lifted the blankets and sheets up from the bottom, and dove headfirst into the bed from there. All I could feel now was Tommy Boy coming up the middle of my bed under the sheets, between me and Maj. It was a funny feeling, him wriggling up trying to meet us out the top of the sheets where our heads were. When he did pop out, he was all smiles, and his eyes were big and round like saucers. He hadn't slept at all. He'd still been downstairs, partying with some folks, when he heard the scream Maj had let out and ran up to check on me. Tommy was the cutest.

I'll admit, this small stint of my life was fun. And I do not regret any of it, but I couldn't handle it all. It was too much partying for even me. It was going to lead me down the wrong road if I wasn't careful. I knew that. I could tell. Each day I felt it more, and that was the good thing. I've always talked to myself and made sure to check in with myself in that way. Thankfully, because no one else was checking in on me.

That arrangement and big apartment room-mate lifestyle lasted one month for me. You'd think that was short, and it was, but to me it felt like a year. The partying didn't cease from the second we took the key to the second I left.

Brad had lost his longtime weekend performer Daryl. One Friday morning, after another successful ladies night at CP, he called me in to speak with him. We decided to take on the full weekend performances together as a duo, like we were doing Thursdays. Now, we'd do it on Saturday and Sunday as well. He told me I could stop working in the kitchen at Icon so I could practice and be more focused on my singing career. Brad said he'd pay me enough so I'd be comfortable. And he did. He paid me a hundred and fifty dollars per night to start, and I was now singing for him three nights per week. I could get my own place. And that's exactly what I did.

I don't think anyone at the house was surprised when I told them I had to move out. I know Tommy Boy wasn't, for sure. The girls seemed a little more perturbed, but they found someone to take over my bedroom and pay my share of the rent right away, so it worked out. Since Sharon was the professional, the lease was in her name, so i didn't have to get out of that either.

I started playing with Brad every weekend and focusing intently on my music. I decided to put the drugs and drinking and partying to rest for a bit. Brad was giving me a big opportunity, and I had to take care of myself to ensure I did it all right, and did it all well. That was important to me. I didn't want to blow this. I wanted to sing and perform and get my shit together. That was what I had come here to do, after all. So, I cleaned up.

I got a new apartment on Gilmour Street, right behind Steamworks for Men, the bathhouse that Brad owned, and two blocks away from CP in the other direction. It was perfectly located, was only five hundred dollars a month, and I'd be by myself. I could handle it on my own, and I was ready to live alone. I was tired of roommates, of partying. All the drugs and everything that came with this hectic, downtown, gay lifestyle.

One funny thing was that, the entire month I lived in that drug house, Miss Carole never visited. It was a good thing. She wouldn't have liked those roommates. She wouldn't have fit in with that crowd at all, and it would have stressed me out. She wouldn't have understood why I liked it. She was a big drinker, but drugs were not her scene.

I'm quite fine with the few bumps of coke I did back then. It was always clean, and I never had one bad trip, ever. It seems in life that I always dabbled at the precipice of the wildest sides, but never went over fully. I have angels watching over me. That's what I believe.

I'll never forget Franky's on Frank Street, though, or sweet Tommy Boy.

21

THE CLEANER

I was performing Thursday through Saturday at CP, and had even started hosting a karaoke night at Icon on Wednesdays. Add that to weekly practices with Brad, and I was working all the time, and I loved it.

My weeks looked like that for about three years straight. I was very content with my schedule, and it turned out to be tons of fun. Thursday nights, I performed with Brad in the Silhouette Lounge for ladies night, to a crowd of mostly women. Fridays and Saturdays, we performed in the Silhouette Lounge again, but for the CP regulars—mostly gay men and a couple of fag hags—and all the Centretown drop-ins. Sundays I would rest or go hang out at CP. Or Brad and I would practice, if my voice could handle it after a long weekend of singing. Otherwise, we'd practice Tuesday afternoons, which would give me a full two days before I needed to sing all night again.

We performed from ten p.m. until two a.m. every night that we played at the Silhouette Lounge. There were always people sitting at the tables waiting when we'd walk in at ten. There were also always people there right until two in the morning. There's nothing worse than playing to an empty room but regardless of whether I was performing to crowd of fifty, or one, I always gave them everything I could.

I loved performing every night with Brad. We had grown very close through our intimate musical partnership, learning to read, and respond to each other's timing, rhythms, and souls. Him on his piano, staring at me all night, watching my every move, and me entertaining the crowds. Each set, Brad would give me a four-to-eight-minute break by playing a couple of Elton John or Billy Joel songs on his piano. He was an excellent, sweet, soft singer, with a gentle tone and solid sound, always on key.

It was nice, too, when I'd get to sing with him. Sometimes, when he'd sing a Billie Joel song, I'd pop back over to my mic and do some harmony with him. He mostly covered solo piano performers who never used backup vocals, so I didn't get as many opportunities to sing backup with Brad as I would have liked.

It was a steady and regular pace for me for those three years. Living only two blocks away down a small alleyway from CP and, pretty much door-to-door, it was simple and convenient. I had my regular diner on the corner, and Brad across the street, at Steamworks, since he lived in an apartment above it during the week.

On weekends, Brad and Donald, his partner, lived at their house in Wakefield, Quebec. They didn't make it out there as much as Brad wanted, but they'd go once a week or so during the summers.

Donald wasn't around much in the winter months. The story was that he would go to Thailand to get hair plugs, but I never knew if that was true. All I know is that, for about half the year, I never had to look at his miserable face, and I loved it.

Brad and I got even closer during the months when Donald was away.

I also got quite close to Brad's second. He was a gorgeous, fun-loving man who would come and hang out in our piano lounge, every single show, then leave with Brad at the end of the night. Brad loved him, too, I could tell. Not a gushy kind of love, but solid, peeking over and seeing him there, leaving with him each night, kind of love. I loved that man, too, and we grew close. He was so sweet and nice, and he'd come grab me when Brad would sing one of his gay ballads, and he'd dance with me, close. He'd waltz with me, like my dad used to do. Until one day, that ended.

I wasn't there, but I heard the story from the staff at CP. One time, when Donald came home from Thailand, someone must have ratted Brad out, because Donald waited and watched and snuck around and spied on them. He saw Brad's friend, and, at the end of the night, he picked a fight with him. He fought loudly and publicly with him in front of many of the staff and regulars.

"Don't think you're going to take what's mine!" That's what I was told Donald yelled.

Then, he shoved Brad's friend down some stairs. The man didn't come back for quite some time. I heard he'd been hurt in that fall. Everyone talked about the incident for a while after. Brad was sad. He didn't talk about it, but I could see. There was a real feeling of dread when Donald was around after that. You know what, though? The next winter, after Donald left for Thailand, guess who came back? Yep, Brad's friend.

It was all so gay and drama-filled. I loved it. It made me feel like less of a drama queen myself, since I always seemed to have one thing or another going on with some Dyke.

Brad and I were confidantes. I told him everything and he told me … everything about some things. He was too loyal to Donald to tell me much about them and their dynamics, but everyone could see it, so we didn't need to talk about him. In fact, I did my best to never mention his name. I couldn't stand him. He was smug, misogynistic, narcissistic, and a good-looking white man. He thought he was a martyr, but he was a right asshole.

~

I got close to the regulars at CP, as well. It would have been hard not to. It was like a giant house with a big family in it. There was this one regular named Gary, a slight man with a pinched face and deeply set inquisitive eyes. I thought he looked a lot like Mick Fleetwood. He would sit at a little table right outside the door into CP, under the awning. As you walked up the stairs, you'd see a little, round table with a chair there, and that was Gary's table. That's where he was every day when CP opened, and he'd be right there for hours. If he wasn't there, like if it was snowing or cold or raining, he would be at a similar table just inside the place, across from the bar.

Gary was always reading the paper, which he did from front to back. Like, all day. It never mattered what time of day I saw Gary; he was always reading the paper. It should have dawned on me that it couldn't take this guy all day to read a paper, but it didn't. I was forever distracted with my own shit.

I could walk by him at two p.m. and he'd be reading it. Then at eight p.m., he'd still be reading it. I didn't think anything of it for months; I just thought that was Gary. I found out later, though that Gary wasn't reading the paper; he was using it as a prop, or disguise, if you will. He was selling pot to everyone at CP. And so the Purse came in and out selling cocaine; and Gary had his reliable "newsstand."

I often wondered where everyone was getting their pot. It goes to show you how solid and loyal they all were. Even the boys, my friends and workmates at CP, didn't tell me what Gary was up to. In fact, they would take my money, run away for ten minutes, then come back with pot for me. I never knew where they got it. But, we'd be right upstairs from Gary. I laughed so hard when I finally figured it out.

Gary would always put his paper down in front of him and look over his glasses to greet me. Every time I came into CP or walked up the stairs to go inside, Gary greeted me. Then, one day, I came in, sat down and stared at him, smiling. He pulled his paper down.

"Good day, young person," he said. "You're sitting here? You never sit here."

Gary was in his late sixties at the time, already retired, a grey-haired, older man. I was still only in my twenties, so that was how he greeted me. I sat there grinning at him. I didn't say a word. I just stared at him.

Until he said, "So you figured it out? Good for you. Now get going. I'm busy reading my paper. You're a distraction."

Then he pulled his paper down again, looked at me, and we both smiled. He never liked anyone sitting at his table too long, because it would get in the way of people coming to buy pot. The fact that I didn't know the true role of the "newsstand" for so long still makes me laugh.

I got up, left, and, like the other staff members at CP, never said a word about Gary to anyone. He knew it, too. He started to like me a lot more as the weeks went by after that. I guess I had turned into another member of the CP family who not only kept his secret, but now went to him for pot, for myself and others. I had become aware, and a great customer.

Gary was sweet and funny and had an old man sense of humour that I liked a lot. I'm sure it was because he was gay, but we got along extremely well. He was so discreet about his business, I figured he was safe.

But, doesn't someone rat Gary out one day. He was picked up by the cops right there outside of CP, at his little table. They showed up, put him in cuffs, and took him away. I heard about it afterwards. It all went down pretty fast, as I was told. It happened right as the bar was opening up.

Gary must have been set up. The cops showed up right at two p.m., when CP opened, and exactly when Gary would set up his table for the day. It was the perfect time for them to bust him; he'd have had the most quantity at opening.

I was at home in my apartment. I had broken things off with a girlfriend I'd been with for a year or so. We'd hated each other but had stayed together because, well, that's what people do sometimes. We had finally broken up, and I'd gotten my own place again this time, near the corner of MacLaren and Elgin. It was a nice, three-storey, apartment building, and I was on the main floor. Entering through the side door of the building, I was the third door on the left.

My windows were ground-level, and when I stood in my apartment, my head would be at the level of the sidewalk outside. That's only important because it's a reason that living there, and that aspect of living there, got gross on many levels. Elgin Street used to be called the Straight Meat Market. It was a street where young, straight people would go to the bars, get utterly loaded, then hang all over Elgin Street at night, being, mostly, young, drunk, straight dudes. It wasn't a place or a street where the gays hung out a lot. But it was close enough to our area.

At night, after the straight bars would close and the young men would be walking around, I would often find one of them pissing against my apartment windows or building. I'd literally look out my window and see some drunk, straight guy pissing. That's what it was like living in a ground-level apartment next to Elgin Street in the nineties. So gross.

But, the location was amazing, with a corner store only feet away, and a pharmacy and all kinds of bakeries and shops, a Chinese food restaurant; there was everything on Elgin. That kind of made up for the grossness of the pissing straight men.

So, I was sitting in my apartment. It was nearly three p.m. and I had a few hours before I was supposed to head down to CP for ladies night. I was chilling when my phone rang.

"Hello?"

"Young lady, it's Gary."

"Oh, hi Gary. What's up? Why are you calling?"

"I've been arrested outside at CP. I'm at the police station on Elgin and I need you to do something very important for me."

"Sure, Gary. Anything you need, I'm there."

"I need you to go to my apartment and get all the drugs out of my place before they go and search it. I'm expecting sometime later tonight, by the time we get all of the questioning out of the way. I need you to get it out, Elaina."

"How will I get in?"

"I've called my landlord and told him I'm at the hospital getting a procedure done and forgot that my cleaning lady was coming in today. He said he'd meet you at the building entrance at three."

"That's in fifteen minutes. Holy shit. Okay, I've got this, Gary. Don't worry about anything. Just take care of yourself in there."

I hung up the phone and was on it. Gary knew that I could be trusted. We'd become close. I saw and spoke to him more than I did my own father in the preceding couple of years. He had also seen me take care of all kinds of other shit. Sitting where he sat at CP, he saw everything.

I had this big skirt from something I had done once during Halloween, and I knew where it was. On the floor in my bathroom I had a metal basket with a handle, which I was keeping my toilet paper rolls in. It only took me a few minutes to figure out how I was going to do it all, but I did, and quick.

I put a scarf on my head, and made it look like I had much more hair under it than I did. I put the skirt on and a nice top I had, and I filled my basket with cleaning supplies. It had Windex and Pine-Sol and two rolls of paper towel sticking up out of it. It looked legit.

I walked quickly over to Gary's apartment, which was only one block away. He was also on MacLaren, but closer to CP, between O'Connor and Metcalfe streets. I was between Metcalfe and Elgin, so we were close. I scuttled over to his place in my get-up and met his building caretaker at the front door, just like Gary had said.

I followed the man up to Gary's apartment, which I had been to a few times for tea on weekends. We'd hang out drink a cup of tea and smoke a joint together. It was our thing. I got to share a lot with him during those visits, including a lot about my history with drugs, and all the things I'd done while dealing drugs and being a mule, all of it. He loved how I opened up to him about it, and I loved telling someone, an older person. It almost felt like a confession. That's why he trusted me; he knew my past.

The building super let me into Gary's apartment.

"How long do you think you'll be so I can lock up?" he asked.

"Probably two hours. That's what it usually takes here."

"Okay, I'll come back at five p.m. and lock up after you."

"Great. Thanks so much."

He left and I promptly closed the door behind him. I went into Gary's bedroom, where he told me to go, and opened the trunk at the end of his bed. I pulled out three giant bags of pot. I had three pounds of cannabis. I hadn't thought that part out. I had figured out how to get there fast enough, and my disguise had gotten me in, but I hadn't realized how much pot there was at Gary's place.

A lightbulb lit above my head and I had it. I quickly pulled my shirt up and started to stuff the bags underneath it. Then I used the waist of the skirt to hold them down around my body. It was tight, and I looked about twice my girth around my waist, but this was all I had. I needed to run with it.

I decided I wasn't waiting around for buddy, either. I quickly grabbed my cleaning supplies, and ran down the stairs and out the back door of the apartment building. I walked so fast down the block to my place, my feet barely touched the ground. I got to the side door of my building, unlocked it with my key, and ran to my apartment door. I opened it, whipped around, locked the door, and sank heavily down on the couch like a pregnant woman, stomach sticking out two feet.

"Phew!"

The bags started popping out of my skirt and onto the floor as I sat, and I started to laugh. All by myself in my apartment. I did it. Gary would be so pleased. He wouldn't get busted for any more than the dozen grams they'd caught him with onsite at CP when they arrested him. I felt so proud that I'd been able to help him this way.

Gary had told me that his pension didn't cover all his bills, so he was selling pot at CP to help subsidize his rent and hydro. I believed him. Gary didn't even drink alcohol; he was a teetotaler. I felt he was telling me the truth.

I immediately called Tory and Steph, two Dyke buddies and besties I'd been hanging with on the daily at the time, to come over. They both arrived right away. I filled them in on some of what had happened, showed them my get-up, then brought them into my bedroom to show them my cooler, the giant one that I used during picnics or outside parties. They looked at me and knew something big was up. I probably looked like the cat that caught the canary. They were super eager to see what I was up to. There was always something going on with me.

I opened the cooler up and there they were—three giant bags of pot. Tory and Steph certainly hadn't ever seen that much pot before, and I hadn't either. Not all together at once like that. the cooler was full to the top with bud. They freaked out. Even more so as I told them the rest of story.

We all laughed. They couldn't believe I'd jumped to it like that, made it happen, saved Gary's ass, and put my own on the line.

The best part was that Gary gave me one-third of that pot as a thank you. I didn't have to buy pot for a year or so after that. The Dykes would all come to my apartment and smoke joints. It was so fun, and we'd tell the story to ourselves over and over and laugh.

22

BOTTOM'S UP

Brad and I had become very well known in the queer community in Ottawa. We started getting asked to play other gay bars. It was usually impossible, since they'd of course want us to perform on a Friday or Saturday night, and, well, I was basically owned by CP. It felt that way, anyway, because of my commitment to play with Brad every Thursday, Friday and Saturday to the regulars in the Silhouette Lounge. I was very happy to have taken that on with Brad, but, after about a year, I missed my weekends. I would watch everyone else on theirs, but mine were spent entertaining.

I tried to make Sunday and Monday my weekends. Thankfully, a lot of gay bar industry folk felt the same. We would often meet up and find ourselves out together on a Sunday or Monday, all propped up at a bar like Bottom's Up, a small gay bar that had opened in Centretown.

Bottom's Up was in the basement of a small building at the corner of Bank and Frank streets, at the very end of the same street Franky's had been on a few years prior, and was owned by the same man. It had male strippers, and was cute and away from the mainstream gay bars and other places we all worked at.

On a Monday night at Bottom's Up, you could find Phil who worked at the Eagle's Nest, Benny and Freddy and others from Icon, DJ Tim from the Oral Grief, Tommy Boy and me, along with all kinds of other gay bar industry folk, all getting drunk together, telling tall tales of our wild weeks in the gay bar industry. It was fun, like a big family outside of work.

During the weekends, though, it was very competitive. We all wanted everyone at our own clubs so we could make the tips and the most money possible. One good thing about those good, ol' years was that all the gay bars were always packed then. We all made excellent money and tips, which was probably why we got along so well.

Back before the internet and dating apps and Grindr and all of it, gay bars were full every night they were open. Sure, most were only open Thursday to Sunday, but they were packed every one of those nights.

It was where you went as a gay person to find love, laughs, and "your people." It was community the second you walked into any one of those spaces. Each had their regulars that made that individual gay bar feel like a family. Grandpa was always sitting at the bar, same place, same time, etc.

One Monday night at Bottom's Up, the entire gang of us were talking way too loudly at each other, getting excited telling stories like we'd do together after a hectic weekend of little sleep and lots of work.

"Wouldn't it be great if we had some entertainment here for our industry nights?" said Benny.

They all looked at me.

"But, wouldn't that mean I wouldn't get *my* industry night?" I said.

They all laughed. I shrugged it off. But, they were serious and didn't let it die.

The next day, I got up and called Carrington, the owner of Bottom's Up. We worked it out for him to have me play with my band down there for industry night the next Monday.

I had been meeting these new musicians who would come by CP with their instruments and join Brad and me in the piano lounge. We were always open to people joining us, and some did it so much that a few of them became part of a band I formed, called Elaina and the Chain. We had started playing bigger Pride shows and big stage events with this full band. I knew they'd be into playing a fun industry night, too.

I wanted to surprise everyone. I had Sundays off, so at least I could relax and take one day off after singing all weekend. I also had Tuesdays off, so I'd be able to rest after the industry night. It all worked out in my head, so I made it happen.

I didn't realize it would happen more than once, but it did. Brad was totally supportive of it. It was an industry night for him, too. But, above all, it didn't interfere with any of the singing I did for him.

I told the band, and everyone was indeed into it. We showed up at Bottom's Up around six p.m. to set up. There were a couple of guys already at the bar talking to Carrington, who didn't work the bar, but who must have been expecting us. All the men were intrigued and checking us all out as we brought our music equipment into the place.

It was like a tennis match, watching them watching us. Then they saw Brad; everyone knew Brad. Well, every gay man knew Brad. They all started talking, and Brad chatted it up with them. Now they were getting excited, and I started to hear some rumblings. Before that, I'd assume they were wondering what the Dyke was doing there. You see, Bottom's Up, like CP, was strictly a gay men's bar, outside of The Purse showing up to feed the regulars their

cocaine. And maybe DJ Tim, the odd fag hag, and myself. Other-
wise, this was a gay men's bar. It was a gay men's strip club, too.
Dykes weren't that interested in going there, or to a place called
Bottom's Up.

We were all set up and sitting around the bar, having a drink and
talking, when the industry folk started to show up. It got the
wildest when Benny arrived, of course. I wasn't seeing him as
much those days. We both had such busy schedules. I had also
wanted to surprise him, so I hadn't told him. And he was indeed
pleasantly surprised.

"Oh, my lucky fucking day off," he exclaimed when he came in
and saw Brad and me. Then, as he caught sight of Brad's big,
digital piano his face lit up as he figured out that we were going to
be playing tonight. I know I have gone on about Benny's charisma,
but it isn't misplaced – he emotes with the exaggeration of a
cartoon character – a level of intensity that always captivated me.

It wasn't long before the band and I got up and into position and
began our first set. I started it off with *Go Your Own Way*, a major
Fleetwood Mac number, fast and energy-filled, and very meaningful to the queers. Going our own way was pretty much what
we were all doing, and the connection was never lost. The crowd
all yelled and cheered.

We kept the energy high. I wanted to wow them all, and I figured
they deserved to be entertained, and to have a wicked night. Also,
because the industry folks were always working their own bars on
the weekend, most of them had never even seen me perform.
They'd heard about me, though, so it was a special event on many
levels.

I performed a lot of the Fleetwood Mac classics, but threw in a
bunch of old rocking songs I used to do, and the band followed
along. They were all so talented, it truly didn't matter what I
decided to do; they'd follow me, perfectly.

I kept the energy high for the entire first set. I sang some Concrete Blonde, another favourite band of Benny's. We sang *Rocket Man* by Elton John, which was a big Brad number. We did all our big anthem songs, and we played and played. The first set was about ninety minutes long. That was on purpose, all part of me wowing my local industry peers.

When I took my first break, it was like I had just started playing all over again, as every industry person in attendance came up to me and was so over the moon about my talent and what they had just experienced. They were delighted to have experienced us live themselves, after hearing so much about us.

These people were all entertainers, as well, only a different kind of entertainment. We had mutual respect for each other. Trust me, bartending in the nineties in gay bars was very much entertainment. You dressed up for the part. You were on, and on and on. Always *on*. You had to be, if you wanted to make the most of your night and get the most tips you could. It was a show, for sure, and I respected it greatly.

I put on a killer performance with my band that night. I remember it very well. I was at the top of my game vocally, and had tons of energy. It had been a good weekend at CP and my Sunday had been super chill. I was so primed for this night, and from all accounts it was a great time for them, too. Everyone was up on their feet dancing the entire time we played. The dance floor was full of my friends, people I knew and had met who were all bartenders, door people, coat check folks, bar cleaners, bus boys. Even some of the go-go boys were in attendance.

At close to midnight, when I was finishing up my second and last set, they all were yelling to Carrington, thanking him, saying how great it was to have us there for industry night, and how we should do this every Monday night. That's when Brad and I looked at each other and grinned. It was a "hopefully you're thinking what I'm thinking" moment.

I told Carrington afterwards that I'd come have a beer with him later that week and chat about it, and he smiled.

We started packing up our gear and, of course, all of both Brad's and my industry buddies helped. We had our shit packed and out of there in about ten minutes, one-quarter of the time it would normally take us. That worked out very well, too. The deal with Carrington had been that we'd come in and play the early part of industry night, until midnight, so he could still host his male strippers and male revue show after our performance. He got two nights worth of programming in one. We did it a couple more times, once every couple of months for about year, before Bottom's Up went … bottom's up, unfortunately.

There had been some issue with the landlord and Bottom's Up needed to close. I can remember everyone feeling so sad about it, and especially sad for Carrington, who had done such a great job of giving us all options outside of Icon, CP, and the Eagle's Nest. He was a wonderfully nice man, who we all liked and wanted to support.

Carrington had sold Franky's on Frank a few years before, when the unaffordability of construction needed to bring the building to code forced him to sell it. Then he opened Bottom's Up, and it was great until it closed. Carrington was an important part of Ottawa's queer community back then, and an even more important part for all the gay industry workers at the time. He gave us our place away from our places. I'll never forget Bottom's Up, or Carrington. Plus, I met Tommy Boy at Franky's, so that gave the location a close place in my heart, as well.

I reached out to Carrington recently to make sure my information and timelines were correct for this book, to find out that he, too, was writing. He had published a book of fiction, a novel, and was working on a new one. It made me so happy for him. What a lovely way to retire after years of hard work in and for Ottawa's gay community.

23
___

THE CENTRETOWN BANDIT

I've mentioned The Purse a lot. She had, to me at least, the perfect cover for a coke dealer, especially a coke dealer to the gays. She was a woman, and a good-looking woman. No one suspected her, and, if anyone like a police officer ever saw her coming in or out of a place, they would think honestly that she had found herself in the wrong place. She was always so quick to go in and out, I'm sure that's what anyone would think. "Oh, that sweet woman must have gone into that gay bar, but then realized it, and that's why she rushed out of there."

Then, of course, there were all of us who knew her quite well. You didn't have to buy cocaine off her to know her; she literally talked to everyone. She was always speaking a mile a minute, and was usually in a good mood, which I liked about her.

She'd come downstairs at CP often, because that's where the bathrooms were, just across from the Silhouette Lounge. That was where the majority of coke deals went down, and where most people did their coke, on the top of the toilet tank covers. As it was directly across from my piano lounge, we had all sorts of characters stopping into our venue all the time.

She'd be doing her business, or lines, in the women's bathroom, then pop into our piano lounge. She'd sip on a drink of some kind, always in a glass, and stand there, swaying usually, but never standing still. She'd watch a song, maybe, but that was it. She was gone again.

She asked me once if I wanted to do a line, but I said no. I told her I didn't do that, not because I didn't. I did, though only once in a while, on my days off, now; not much at all anymore. I told her I didn't do it, though, because I didn't want her coming around me like that. Everyone knew who she was and what she was doing in the gay bar, and I didn't want them thinking I was one of her "clients," because I wasn't. So, the audience thought she was what they all were—a fan who stopped in on their night out, to catch a set or a song.

The Purse was busy. She was going to all the gay bars, not just CP. She was over at the Eagle's Nest, which was rampant with the stuff and people doing it, but also Icon. And she'd deliver to Steamworks, the bathhouse. They wouldn't let her in, but she'd meet the guy at the counter, deliver to him, and he'd deliver inside to whomever. He was a friend of mine, a drag queen by night and a bathhouse door entrance guy by day. Steamworks was a wild place.

The Purse was busy. The coke business was so busy, in fact, and there were plenty more people providing cocaine in downtown gay establishments than just her. Cocaine was such a common and wildly popular drug in the nineties.

The other well-known and popular coke dealer at the time, in those spaces, was a gay man named Dorian, he was tall and thin and dressed like the stereoptype of a seventies pimp, wide brim hat with a feather, leather trenchcoat and the likes. I would speak with him on my breaks. He was very well-spoken, and sounded educated to me. He had this floor-length, black, leather coat he would wear. He was always very well dressed, with proper slacks and fashion shoes, like classy men's loafers.

He, too, had a great cover. He looked like a rich, gay man, not necessarily someone who would be dealing cocaine. But he was. He didn't do the large circuit The Purse did. He only covered the strictly gay men's spaces. He told me once that he didn't want to be running all over the city, when he knew the people doing the most of the drug were gay men.

Dorian had pretty much fully cornered the bathhouse market, because he could get past the doorman, who usually took his cut of each order, by the way. If your cocaine had to pass through too many hands to get to you, it was probably half the size when you got it, and half as good. That was the case when guys ordered at the bathhouse; they got what they got. That was why Dorian was popular there. He would bring it right to you.

Same at CP. He had access to the spaces The Purse didn't, like Cell Block, the leather and sex bar on the very top floor of CP. It was a place most people, even people who went to CP for years, never went up to. I loved it up there, and I'd bring women up to make out sometimes. They'd be surprised and in wonder when I'd climb them up the cast-iron wall of steps to get there. It was a loft-like space, dim and sparsely lit. The walls were painted black, the windows were painted black, it was pitch black. The only way you could see at all was by the light coming up from the floor beneath, where the dance floor was. Those lights shone bright enough that you could kind of see where you were walking.

At the very back, there was a blackout room. Inside you'd find steel barrels, and glory holes along the wall. That was Cell Block. But, the best and most important feature of Cell Block was the iron jail bars throughout that entire level. It was completely surrounded by iron bars, all put in by a specialist iron worker. It was meant to resemble jail culture, a huge gay men's fantasy prop at the time.

Brad and I produced a band photo shoot up there once. I still have these wicked black-and-white photos of Brad, me, and my band Elaina and the Chain, all behind bars up in Cell Block. I don't look at those photos a whole lot. Three of my band members are not alive anymore, so it hurts. But, about once a year, they come out and I feel it all.

I got to know Dorian a wee bit better than The Purse, because he was a huge fan of mine and Brad's. He would get his business out of the way first, so that he could enjoy the entire night with us down in the Silhouette Lounge. He would come and grab a table, and order his fancy gin and tonics, and people would come sit with him at his little table. To get what they wanted, Dorian would make them sit and have a drink with him and watch me sing. That was so funny to me. He'd wink at me while I was on stage as I watched him slide his hand across his table to the other person, who would slide their hand to meet his. The swap would take place with no one the wiser, except me.

From the stage, I saw everything. People in the crowd didn't understand the power of being sober and being on one side of the place while everyone was on the other. I literally saw everything. They were all partying, but they also assumed I was so into my songs and putting on a good show that I wasn't paying attention to what they were all doing. But, that was not the case.

I saw everything they were all doing. I saw every deal. Every pick-up. Every fight and/or heated argument under the music. Every make-out session, and every spoiled first date. I just did. I was sober and, honestly, bored most of the time, just singing. I'm also a multitasker, so singing a song and watching what was going on in the room wasn't hard.

Brad saw lots, too. He never said anything about the drug dealers; it was so embedded into the culture that no one said anything.

Dorian and The Purse knew each other. In fact, I'm sure I

remember him telling me they got their drugs from the same dealer, another gay man who owned a different club that had recently opened down the Street. He was a great guy, whom I liked a lot, and had been the dealer at CP for years until he opened his own place. It was a gorgeous place, and he had some funders who I think had deep connections to money, and others, obviously, to drugs. Possibly, the money and the drugs were from the same connections.

Dorian and The Purse got along great. You'd think they'd fight or be at odds or competitive, at least, but nope. Clearly there was enough of a demand to create room for them both. They were friends and would often take each other into the washroom to do a line together. I can only describe their relationship as being like "industry folk" to each other. That was how they acted when they met up. Always a big hug, talking like they were catching up, and friendly. They were doing the same thing and had the same challenges, and I'm sure they discussed it all, because I saw them chatting nose-to-nose a few times. Maybe they were discussing strategy; I don't know.

One day, the cops came into CP, and were walking around all the floors and looking here and there. They searched all through the main space at CP, then went out into the backyard, and to the side of the building. Then they spoke to the bartender and left.

Of course, commotion started among everyone about how the cops had been at CP. They were all asking why. The bartender didn't know, exactly, but he said they had been looking for someone. They had told him they were looking for a guy who had robbed a bank. They said they had reason to believe he might be at CP. That was code, we all understood, for them thinking the guy was gay.

The news got around very fast, and we were all, like, what bank robber? Who is it? Why are they looking here? That night, I heard all about it at my bar downstairs at CP. Everyone was talking about the cops who had come in earlier looking for a fugitive. We were all laughing about it, not taking it seriously. It was simply the drama of the day.

The next day, though, the News, which I listened to each morning while waking up, mentioned it. I loved listening to the radio when I first got up each day. It helped me align myself with the weather and shit happening in the city. They mentioned that there had been two bank robberies in Centretown, and that the police were actively looking for the robber, a man said to be in his early forties. He was believed to have been seen recently in Centretown.

Okay, I thought. That's what they were doing at CP. Oh well, that doesn't affect us in any way. I thought, that's some guy robbing banks, and discarded it all together. I was sure it was no one I would ever know.

That night, I went back to CP to play my show with Brad, and everyone was talking about the Centretown Bandit. I was, like, who? Everyone was talking about this man who was robbing banks in Centretown, and how the cops had been to the Duke of Somerset, Icon, Steamworks, and all the bars and restaurants in Centretown, looking for clues and gathering information about the guy. I'll admit it became big news around CP and Centretown. For a couple of weeks, it was all anyone could talk about.

"The Centretown Bandit." That was what everyone started calling him. I liked the name. Kudos to whoever named him that, because it was pretty exciting. I wouldn't at all be surprised if the Bandit had given himself that name.

I heard the next night that the cops had been back in CP again, and that, during this visit, they had mentioned they suspected a gay man was robbing the banks. They asked the bartenders to look out for a man they had a blurry photo of, taken from one of the banks he had robbed. But no one recognized the guy. I heard it was too blurry to tell. You couldn't see anything.

The radio news was talking about it all the time now. It turned out he had robbed another bank in Centretown. I thought, everyone has been talking about this guy robbing banks in Centretown, and yet he's able to rob another bank in Centretown in the meantime? Weren't the banks all expecting him by now? Why weren't they putting security into the banks in Centretown for the week? He'd already hit two banks, and now a third?

It became a game of when would they find the Centretown Bandit. The feeling and tone, around CP at least, was that this guy was a Superman. Robbing banks in Centretown, not getting caught, and out on the lamb? A gay man? In the Cell Block culture and others, he became a kind of a superhero.

I was at home in my apartment on Gilmour one evening. My girlfriend at the time worked nights, and I was off, hanging out at my place before I would head down to CP to visit my buds and shoot the shit. My phone rang. It was Dorian, calling me from the bar at CP.

"Hello, beautiful. It's Dorian."

"Hey! How are you, brother? How did you get my number?"

"I begged Jeff at CP to give it to me. Well, I fixed him up for it, of course."

"Of course you did," I laughed. "What can I do for you?"

"I'm hoping I can pop by your place and have a chat with you. Maybe a cup of tea?"

"I don't have tea, but I can make you a coffee. Come on over. I was just chilling. It's my day off."

"I know, darling. That's why I called you. I was thinking it was your day off and possibly you were hanging at your place. I remembered you saying it was behind Steamworks. May I please come over?"

"For sure, brother. Buzz me at 504 when you get here and I'll let you in."

"I'll see you in five minutes, my gratitude darling."

He always spoke to me like we were in a nineteen fifties movie. He was the ultimate gentleman, truly he was. He tipped me at the piano lounge every time he sat for a set; he would never leave without tipping. He'd strut up to my tip jar on the piano, lower his hand into the giant brandy snifter, and put in his usual twenty, sometimes a hundred dollar bill, or sometimes a gram of cocaine. He'd do it and wink at me, every time.

Brad would look up at me and laugh and smile with his twinkly eyes. To me, it was a sign that he was pleased the men there were so taken with me.

Dorian was very generous with me. He'd give me coke every time I saw him, whether I wanted it or not.

"If you don't want it," he'd say, "give it away and be a superstar."

He was right. Each time I gave any of the boys my gram or half of coke, they were ecstatic. People didn't give away drugs like that back then, but I did. They were free, and I didn't always feel like doing them. I'm lucky; my relationship with hard drugs was like that, always, without exception. It was a non-issue for me. Like I said, I was lucky.

I put the coffee on and waited for Dorian to buzz up. It didn't take long at all; he was literally just down the street. I let him in. When he arrived at my door, he was as cool as a cucumber, as usual. He had his leather coat on, with slicked hair and clean fingernails. I'll tell you, this gay had his shit together. He was clean and sparkly. It mattered to him, being put together, and it showed.

Me, on the other hand, I was totally chillin'. He showed up and it was my day off and I was at home. I had cut-off long johns on as makeshift shorts, and a hole-riddled T-shirt, but that didn't stop him from greeting me with, "Good morning, beautiful" when I opened the door and invited him in. He looked around my small place and complimented me on it. We sat at my kitchen table and had coffee, something I had never done with anyone before at this apartment.

"So, what can I do for you, Dorian? Why are you here?"

"Oh, darling. I'm in trouble and I need a place to hide out for a couple of days. If you'll have patience with me, I'll explain everything."

"I've got nothing but time, friend," I said.

Let's face it, I was totally intrigued now, but I still didn't get it. It still didn't smack me in the face.

"I'm the Centretown Bandit," he said.

"What?" I started laughing so much I nearly fell off my kitchen chair. I laughed so hard, my eyes were watering. I couldn't control myself. He'd been there at CP while we all discussed it. He had been part of our conversations about the bandit. I laughed and laughed, and then I stopped and looked at him.

"Oh, you're good," I said. "How in hell have you not gotten caught? What are you doing? How are you getting away with all of these robberies?"

"Darling, you won't believe it, but I literally slip them a note saying I have a weapon and to pass me their money, and then they give it to me and I run off."

"What?" I was listening to him intently, and I was awed to hear about it all.

"Yeah. But what's funny is the most dangerous thing I have ever had on me while robbing any of those banks was a nail file."

We both start laughing hard again. I couldn't handle it. It was all so hilarious and exciting to me. A nail file; he had robbed all those banks with a nail file.

"What are you going to do?" I asked.

"Turn myself in, eventually. But, I have to pay some people off first."

"How do you plan on doing that?"

"I have some work to do in the next two days, but the cops are now looking for me everywhere. They've been to my apartment, and they know it's me."

"So, you're a fugitive?"

"Yes, Elaina. I'm a fugitive."

"Holy shit."

"Yes. I was hoping I could stay here with you for two days. I'll have these guys paid off in two days and I'll turn myself in," he said.

"May I please use your phone?" he asked. "I want to call my sister. She's been very worried. The photos are out now, and they all know it's me. The last bank I robbed got a very good likeness of me on its cameras, and it's all out. My sister is very upset."

"I bet she is. You can tell her to come here and see you if she wants."

And that's what he did. He told his sister to come to my place, and she did right away. I think his family was very concerned.

Dorian's sister, Tammy, was the loveliest woman. She was a nice-looking, blonde, average, but a lovely, smart, and caring woman. She had her shit together, too. She was married and had children, and was sweet and loving. She was so kind to me, and thanked me so much for being a friend to Dorian.

Later, Dorian said he had to go out for a bit. He was going to head back to Steamworks, a place he felt safe. The cops didn't like to go inside bathhouses. That would change.

Tammy decided to stay and have coffee with me and talk. We hit it off right away. She filled me in on Dorian's life a bit, and what had gone down with him. It turned out he had been acting out after a terrible break up with his husband. He had been in a married, committed, relationship. Then something bad had happened and they broke up. They'd owned a house together, and a retail shop. They'd had a nice gay life together, until it ended.

I guess the loss of all of that had sent Dorian over the edge. He'd started doing harder drugs, first cocaine and then using needles. He got mixed up with the people who dealt it, then started dealing it himself to keep his own habit alive. Then one thing led to another. Now he owed these people so much money for the coke, he'd started to rob banks to pay them off, or they were going to hurt him.

This was all coming from Tammy, this sweet, hetero, straight-laced woman. I was shocked. It told me right away that she was Dorian's safe place, his confidante. He'd told her everything. I was glad she'd shared all of that with me, as well. It made Dorian more real to me, more of a person and less of a character.

Tammy stayed with me for a couple of hours. We talked and became quite close. She stayed until Dorian came back. He was a little freaked out when he did. He had snuck out the back door of Steamworks just in time, as the cops were over there searching the place right now.

Dorian said he needed to lay low and not leave anymore for a day or two. Tammy looked at me.

"Are you sure he can stay here with you?" she asked.

"Yes, I'm sure," I said, looking at them both.

Dorian did stay with me for two days, and it was chill. He was a lovely guest. He was helpful and cheery, considering what was going on and what was to come.

On Thursday, when it was time for me to head to CP for ladies night, I said good bye to Dorian and he was sad to not be able to come to CP as well. That night when I got home though, Dorian was gone.

He did leave me a kind note saying thanks. It was filled with love, but said it was getting close now, and he didn't want to incriminate me further. So, he was gone to the Club Ottawa Baths. He'd heard the cops hadn't been there yet; I guess because that bathhouse was in Hintonburg, not Centretown, and they were focusing on Centretown.

People had started talking now, and pointing Dorian out to the cops. It was all coming to a head. At CP, it was all anyone could talk about. The cops had been there again that day. And this time, the bartender told me, they'd asked about me.

"What do you mean they asked about me?"

"They asked about the woman who sang in the basement," he said. "If you knew Dorian and what your relationship was with him."

"Oh my god. What did you tell them?"

"I told them you were a Dyke and only here to sing and didn't really know any of the people here. Just the entertainer. That seemed to appease them."

"Thanks, sweetie!"

"No problem. But you know where Dorian is, right? He's not with you?"

"Hell no. What do I look like?"

With that, I walked around the corner and down to the piano lounge like it was nothing. But I was worried, scared for how it would all go down.

The next morning was a Friday, and Tammy called me first thing. I woke to the phone ringing. She was frantic. She'd heard from Dorian, but he'd been a mess. He'd been talking nonsense and scaring her. She said she needed to see him. She told me he was still at the Club Ottawa Baths and asked if I would go there with her.

"The Ottawa Baths is a strictly gay men's bathhouse, sweetie. They aren't going to let us in there."

"But, I have to see him, Elaina. We have to get him out of there. It's time he turn himself in."

"Okay. Come and get me," I said.

"Give me twenty minutes and I'll be there, Elaina. Thank you."

I hopped into the shower, got dressed, and headed outside to meet Tammy. I had enough time to have a cigarette, then she pulled up at the front of my building.

We drove over to the Club Ottawa Baths, which were under a giant bingo hall in Hintonburg. Tammy parked out front. We had discussed it in the car and decided that I'd go in, use my charms, and try to get him out of there.

I went in. This gay guy I knew from CP, Alan, was at the door. He looked at me weirdly.

"What are you doing here?" he asked.

"I'm here for Dorian. His sister is out in the car and we need to take him with us."

"You can't come in here," he exclaimed.

"Listen. You have three options, Alan. You either let me in to get

Dorian, and I do it quickly and painlessly and we leave with him; I make the biggest fucking scene here and bust my way in to get him; or the cops show up and raid the entire place to get him."

I was serious and using my Dyke confidence. He believed me.

"Buzzzzzzz," the door clicked.

"He's in the third room on the right," said Alan.

I went inside and down the hall. When I got to the third door, I knocked. I didn't hear anything, so I opened the door. Dorian was laying on a little cot. I sat down on the bed with him. He jolted like I was going to kill him, so I calmed him down and softly let him know it was me. We talked quietly until he got his bearings and I could tell him that his sister was outside, worried sick, and wanted to help him turn himself in.

"It's time, Dorian," I said.

He gave me a look of defeat. It was the most depressed I'd ever seen sweet Dorian. He was sad. He knew what was ahead for him, and it was ever so real in that moment.

I got him dressed and walked him past the doorman. I thanked Alan, and he looked at me all mad.

"Don't you dare come back and try intimidating me again, Dyke," he said.

"I won't. Thank you."

Dorian and I walked outside. When he got into the daylight, he squinted his eyes hard, and they watered down his face. The bath-houses are dark places. He'd been in there without going outside for at least two days, and doing all kinds of drugs. We got in the car. Tammy and Dorian worked out the details. We decided together that they'd drop me off at my apartment, so as to not involve me any further. Then they would go to the downtown cop shop on Elgin Street. Dorian would turn himself in with his sister by his side. He'd be with his big sister, a solid community member, a wife and mother. She was going to hold his hand the entire way.

And she did. They arrested Dorian. It was all on the news and everyone was talking about it. The Centretown Bandit had turned himself in. It got out and everyone knew it was Dorian.

People were wildly excited that he had been in their spaces for months as the bandit but no one had known. It would have been entertaining, but I only felt sad for Dorian. It reminded me how, when life's shit hits the fan sometimes, we always have two roads we can walk down: the road to healing or the road to destruction. Unfortunately, sometimes people get so hurt, and feel so bad, that the choice isn't so much of a choice as a reaction. That was the case for Dorian. He was heartbroken, and one thing led to another. The fast lane caught hold of him and that was that: he was inside, doing hard time for robbery.

I don't remember how many years Dorian was actually inside, but he got out eventually. When he did, it wasn't long before he came to find me. I was one of the first people he looked up when he got out. I was running my own festival by then. It had been at least ten years since I'd seen him. But, outside of him aging, he hadn't changed a lot. He was still the same Dorian, just not as wild anymore, you know, older.

He had gotten out early for good behaviour. He'd done some peer work inside, and had started working at a group home for men who'd done time. He was essentially a social worker for incarcerated men now. He'd healed from the loss of his relationship, and had educated himself while inside. He was starting a new life, and I was happy for him.

24

MISS INTERPRET

Brad and I had been singing together downstairs at CP for three years now and things were smooth sailing until I wanted to start a women's music festival. I asked Brad and his partner—who together owned three large, gay businesses in the city—to sponsor it but Donald, Brad's partner, said no. He called me an opportunist for wanting to do something other than sing in his club.

I had been doing the summer music festival circuit, playing at a women's music festival just outside of town, and at other festivals locally. My underwhelming experiences, both as an artist and as an attendee for two years at the area women's music festival, drove me to want to produce one myself. I started pulling together some women to help organize it, and got momentum going. Everyone was into it, except for Brad and Donald.

I had approached them with a serious win-win deal for both of us. They would sponsor it and I would turn a dead night at Icon into a ladies fundraiser night. Donald got angry right away. He didn't see the win on their part at all, and stood up right away and raised his voice and acted mean and controlling. Brad, having no real chance at combatting Donald, gave in.

It ruined our relationship, instantly. I could have tried harder. I could have had more patience and tried a different approach, or given it a couple of days and gone back again. I could have, but I didn't. I'm quick like that. If you hurt me, especially when i feel i've done right by you, I get angry. And when I get angry, I don't make perfect decisions; that's on me. When I get angry, I want to move on and start something new.

I was so disappointed that, after three years of turning their piano lounge around and creating a successful ladies night in a historic gay men's bar, and all the crowds I'd drawn down there, that they'd …. I had thought ….

But no. Donald was not about helping my dreams come true, about supporting my future, and he outright said so. I was insulted. Truly, that's what I was. I had been so loyal to these guys. I had never played other gay bars, despite the multiple offers. I wanted to be loyal to them.

I was sad to not have Brad, at least, return that loyalty. The situation changed everything.

I stopped playing at CP the day after our fight. I pulled all my shit out of that piano lounge. I went down to the recently opened Club Polo lounge and offered the owner the same exact deal that I had offered Donald and Brad. He jumped at my offer. He stood up and was so excited by it, we moved forward with my plans right away. All my fundraisers took place there. We held them the last Sunday of every month for a solid year, until the following summer, when my new festival took place.

I found a spot in Wakefield, a beauty of a location. I had a co-director who helped me pull it all together that first year. She was mostly doing marketing and branding, and I was doing logistics. We pulled it off, and over five hundred women showed up to that festival, with Tegan and Sara as our first-year headliners.

I'd named the festival the Rock City Women's Fest, after a trip to

Sudbury had me driving by the Rock City Auto Wreckers on the Kingsway and a light bulb went off for me. The festival was at a limestone quarry, and I planned on the acts being mostly rock and roll, so it worked.

In year one, we didn't make money. Hell, in year two we wouldn't make money, either. We barely paid all the bills in that first year, and certainly didn't pay ourselves. It was a hard year, with many challenges and much adjustment. But, we did make enough money to encourage us to try it again. So, we started planning year two. I was full-steam ahead, and wasn't going to let anyone stop me.

The first Rock City Women's Fest got some shitty press from men who wanted to come and weren't allowed based on our women only mandate. I was fine with that; we can have all-women's spaces. I had some trans women who wanted to come, too. We had modelled ourselves after other women's festivals at the time and hadn't given too much thought to the language of "born women" and policing of gender those mandates made visible. After year one, and hearing from people that this was actually TERFy—not a term we used back then, but one we definitely use today—it became a debate among my organizing team, who were all lesbians. As I had divided the organization of the festival and preoccupied myself primarily with the logistics of finding space and booking acts, the subtleties around inclusion evaded me in that first year.

"It's a women's festival," they cried.

Added to the critique that trans women justly vocalized, I also just had so many gay male friends who wanted to come – they were, after all, an integral part of the fabric of the queer community that had supported me and allowed me to flourish in Ottawa.

You see, it was a music festival to me first. It was modelled after other women's music festivals, because at the time we were a bunch of Dykes trying to do something we'd never done before, and we'd used the models we had before us.

But, that was wrong. And after the first year, that was driven home for me as folks shared the exclusion our mandate had produced. And I had deeply felt like things were missing at the first event. I told the team that I wanted to open it up to everyone.

"Why can't we be a women's music festival where everyone comes and enjoys women's music?" I said.

It was a very divisive time for the organizing team. My organizers were adamant it stay women-only, and were rigid in who they meant when they said "women." But I had just come off a three-year run of entertaining gay men almost exclusively, of sharing space with drag queens in the entertainment industry. In fact, I had more gay male friends than I had lesbian friends. I couldn't stomach it and though I didn't have the politics, language, or insight I now have, thirty years later, I instinctively lamented the fact that anything I would do would produce exclusion. I demanded we open it up. My co-director left, and the organizing team changed slightly. But I got my way, and we opened it up.

That was a great decision. In fact, even today, when I look at the photos from year one, yeah, it's nice and cool and I see lots of women having fun. But when I look at the photos from year two, it's another story all together. It's beauty.

Year two, we had so many special guests. I had decided to plan one helluva party. So, I opened up our marketing and advertising to the greater gay community, and said, "Everyone is welcome."

To make it even better, I gave tons of tickets away to gay men that I knew, and to all the drag queens. I missed that aspect of gay life the first year.

The second Rock City Women's Fest was way more fun, for so many reasons. The gay men I was organizing the Ottawa Pride festival with came and spent the weekend with their gay male lovers. It was nice to see them enjoying themselves. At one point, I was walking one of the paths through the festival site, and I could see one of the gay male couples in a canoe on one of the lakes onsite. They were smiling, and it was so nice. It was that moment when I fully knew I had done the right thing opening it all up.

I walked over to the stage area, and found Johanna Wright at one of the tables where organizations were promoting their services. She was, and still is, the most iconic trans woman in Ottawa. She's been a founding leader of the trans movement here in town, an activist, role model, teacher, and having her join the festivities was a meaningful demonstration of my festivals ability to listen and adapt. The critiques hadn't been "complaining to complain", as some of the other women had claimed. Folks honestly wanted to come and take part and be queer in community and celebrate women, all women.

The best part was the queens showing up. I had booked a driver and a van to go to Ottawa and get the drag queens I'd hired, and all their gear, and bring them out. At the end of the night, they would be returned home by the same driver and van.

The queens had made it very clear to me they would not be sleeping in tents and we simply didn't have the necessary facilities for them to clean up properly. You can't get your make-up off in a porta-potty. It's not doable.

The queens had requested to come spend the entire night with us, to perform and party. When they were ready, we could get them home. That worked out.

We had Ginette Bobo, Tanya Carding, and Tenille Dysfunction and Mama Judd was the headliner. They showed up in full drag and heels, and we all watched as the van pulled up to the stage with them. It was thrilling for me and all of the people there. We watched each queen disembark from the van, bent in half to get out of the vehicle, since they were so tall.

They were all dolled-up and the moment they were all out of the van the crowd cheered. I don't know if you've ever heard a crowd of Dykes cheering, but it's like being at a football game. It felt like the queens really were royalty and it was all weird and wonderful for them, as well. I watched them all looking around at the scenery and smiling and laughing. They were all so happy. It was still light out when they arrived and they walked around in their heals on the grass until Mama Judd yelled, "I'm going to break my ankle on this grass, Dyke!"

We all laughed. I got the golf cart and put them all in it, and drove them around like royalty for the rest of the night. We drove into the area where hundreds of mostly women, but all kinds of folks now, had tents pitched. I was swerving in and around all the tents, with the queens in my golf cart howling. They were each waving like the Queen of England and being fawned over by all who could get near them. They were the superstars, for sure. They not only livened up the place, but they added some of the "fabulous" that I felt was missing in the first year.

Friday night was a big dance party that year. We had women playing music on the stage until ten p.m. Then we moved the party into the giant tent where we'd had the women vendors all day. It became a killer dance party under that tent, with drag shows well into the night. The next morning, when I got up, I found a couple of people sleeping under that tent, still surrounded by dance party mess. That made me laugh. I had taken off a bit earlier to get some rest after a long day. It was great to see the remnants of a stellar night of drag.

One of the members of my organizing committee who had left as a result of the changes to open things up was a new, good friend of Miss Carole's. She was a cold and resentful toward me, but Miss Carole loved her. I think she was in love with her. Either way, Miss Carole had her eyes set on this woman and she was glued to her for a year or so. Miss Carole stopped staying at my place when she was in Ottawa, and would stay with this woman, instead. It bothered me, and we eventually spoke about it.

Miss Carole was restoring a VW Westfalia van and also a VW Beetle. Restoration was her passion, and a hobby since she'd started making great money with CN. She didn't have anywhere else to spend it. She became a VW collector and was restoring those two vehicles to their former glory. They were great. I loved both of them. Her Bug was lime green, and her van was that iconic yellow. She would drive them both everywhere. I'd always hear her coming, shifting those old standard gears.

She was living in Cornwall now, working the Cornwall station and track for CN. I didn't see her as much anymore. But, she needed to move her Bug to her place in Cornwall from where it was in Sudbury. She could only drive one vehicle, so she called me up and asked if I could come with her to Sudbury on my day off and drive one back for her. I said yes, of course.

We stopped in Sudbury for breakfast before leaving, and we got into it. I told her how sad I was that she was hanging with a woman I could no longer stomach, and who was a user and abuser. I had heard so many stories from other lesbians who had dated her; details of her manipulative, and lying ways. She had a solidly shitty reputation in the community.

I also had something else to talk to Miss Carole about, and I chose that time to do it. I probably shouldn't have, in retrospect. I started to talk to her about her ex, Steph, who was now the new general manager of Rock City. She had been incredibly helpful towards me, and was a great, loyal friend and confidante. Miss Carole wasn't happy to hear any of this.

My bigger issue was that the next Rock City Women's Fest was about to happen in only a couple of months. I asked Miss Carole if she could be cool with Steph and her new girlfriend, Veronica, while attending the festival, so we could all keep the peace. Miss Carole saw it as betrayal. She immediately started to cry and was upset with me.

It wasn't betrayal at all. I wanted to ensure everyone would get along—or not fight, at least—at the festival. There was history there. Steph, who was Miss Carole's ex-girlfriend, was now dating a woman she'd met through Miss Carole. So that hurt. Veronica was a good friend of Miss Carole's from CN, in fact. Miss Carole had brought her to see me perform at CP many times in years past, so I knew her, too. After Steph and Miss Carole broke up, I guess Veronica and Steph started dating. Veronica was a bit of a nervous type. She didn't want to come to Rock City, because she feared shit would go down with Miss Carole. Steph had filled me in on this, and it was in the back of my mind while talking with Miss Carole. I let it all out.

That hurt Miss Carole. She misinterpreted the entire conversation and took it the wrong way, like I had chosen sides. Like I was asking Miss Carole to behave herself and not start a fight with this woman, making Miss Carole out to be the potential problem. That wasn't the case, though. I had been trying to ensure drama wouldn't turn the festival into a lesbian fighting camp. I wanted to keep the peace, but I wasn't picking sides. If I ever did pick sides, I would have picked Miss Carole's, without question.

Our breakfast was ruined by that conversation, and Miss Carole didn't understand my intention. She was hurt. To her, I had been disloyal by even asking her to keep cool with Steph and Veronica. She didn't hide her anger with me.

We drove back to Ottawa, her in her VW Bug and me in her VW van. Without cell phones at the time, we couldn't continue to talk or anything. So we drove, all hurt, the six hours back to Ottawa.

When we arrived in O-town, we hugged, hard. She thanked me and I went back to my apartment in Centretown, having dropped the van off at a parking lot where she was keeping it on Gilmour Street.

Turned out, Miss Carole didn't even come to the second Rock City. She was still pissed. She started dating a new woman, though, a cop in Cornwall. I didn't see Miss Carole much for the next year. I was sore about that. Hell, she had come to Ottawa following me, we were the best of friends, and now it was all broken. I was horribly sad about it.

Smokey came to Rock City that year, though, and brought her girl-friend and kid with her from southern Ontario. We spent the weekend catching up and being together, and it was everything for me. She showed up in the middle of the night. Security knocked on my trailer door.

"You have a friend here from far away."

"Let them in," I barked.

Then, all groggy in my bed, I felt someone sit on the side of it. When I opened my eyes even in the dark of the night, I could see her face full of teeth, smiling at me. She put her newborn son in my bed next to me.

"Joshua," she said, "this is Auntie Miss Elaineous."

I laid there and cried. I needed Smokey that weekend, and she came up and ensured she was with me—wife, kid, and all.

It was Pride 2000, our first Pride in the new millennium, and it was being produced on Bank Street. I was organizing the women's stage. I had Tegan and Sara and a bunch of local Dykes performing on a stage at the corner of Bank and Lewis Street, right around the front of Steamworks.

Miss Carole came with her girlfriend. They came to my stage. I walked out from behind it when I saw them both, and I spent some time with Miss Carole, which was nice. It was different now, though. She was with someone I didn't know, and that was very strange for me. I had always known Miss Carole's girlfriends. Also, she was with a cop, which was a real no-no for me now. It was the first time in over a decade that I hadn't known the woman dating my best friend. It was so odd and wrong, and it felt that way, too. It made me sad.

I was in a miserable relationship at the time, and we sat there across from Miss Carole and her girlfriend, whom I felt so cold with. Unhappy in my own relationship, I felt defeated. We sat at a little table on the street and watched my show for a bit. Then I excused myself and left all three of them sitting there. I couldn't handle it. And when I feel shitty, I leave.

Miss Carole died not long after that. She was killed in a tragic train accident. It took her life in Cornwall, where she had been working for two years. It was right after our only shitty time together ever.

Miss Carole and I had a beautiful friendship for so many years, then it hit this rough patch, and then she was stolen from me. I traveled along with her body to Sudbury. We brought her home to bury her there, among her family. It's been a source of pain and sadness for me for years now, how everything went down prior to her dying. It shouldn't have been that way. I shouldn't have allowed anything to come between us, but I did.

25

NOT A VILLAGE

Today, in 2020, some call Centretown "The Village," but it's so far from being a village, or even the village it once was or sought to be years ago. It's not even a gay area anymore. It's history, that's it. It's like someone took what was happening twenty years ago and tried to make it look like it was happening today. But, it isn't.

As I write this, there is not even one gay-owned business still in Centretown in that gay corridor between Somerset and Frank to my knowledge.

I remember years ago when Brad tried to get the area to acknowledge the queers and make it a village. At that time, in the late nineties, they laughed in his face. Not only did queers fill Centretown streets then, but we patronized all the businesses there, bought all the real estate there, and rented all the apartments there.

Then, twenty years later, completely after the fact, and because the area had died down, they threw up queer banners and painted the crosswalk rainbow colours and put up signs calling it the "The Village." They've been trying to attract a market that long ago disappeared, evaporated, and moved on.

All those other queer businesses had opened up in Centretown originally because Brad had chosen that part of the city to start building up. It was Brad's plan for it to become like Church Street in Toronto; that was always his plan. That's why they had opened a bathhouse along with all the bars they opened. If it was to be a true queer village, it needed a bathhouse.

Brad did a great job of owning and running two highly successful gay bars, but they were more than bars. What do you call a building that has three full and differently themed spaces, on three separate floors, all decorated and branded differently? A building that could see over a thousand people in it in one, single night? I don't know, but that's what they created. Twice. It was like you could find almost everything you needed in the one place, so why go anywhere else. I'm sure that's what they were going for, and it seems brilliant to me, mostly because it totally worked.

When you were at Icon, if you wanted to start upstairs in the dance club, great, you could dance all night. If you got tired and wanted something quieter, you could head to the main floor. There, you had a classy space with tables and chairs, and an open space to hang and talk, and you could order food. If you felt like being entertained, you could come on Wednesdays to karaoke, or go down to the drag show on Sundays, or to Zena's any other night. It was all-encompassing.

CP was similar. Top-floor sexy times, main-floor pub and pool tables, downstairs entertainment.

For one full decade, Brad and Donald's clubs provided the heyday of the queer scene in Ottawa. Coral Reef had been closed for a few years. Franky's was closed. The Eagle's Nest was fine on a Friday, but always too loud and too cramped, being the only gay bar in the Market. It was all about the Centretown hop at the time. That's what a bunch of us called it, as we would hop from one street and gay establishment to the other while living in Centretown.

I loved when I lived on Gilmour, right behind Steamworks. At the corner was the small diner Brad and I often ate breakfast at. It was gay-positive, with a Pride flag outside. Also at that corner, at Bank and Gilmour, was Wilde's, a mostly gay male sex shop. But nice gay boys ran it and wouldn't ever be anything but lovely to the Dykes who might go in, myself included. Upstairs they had video stalls and glory holes.

Across the Street was After Stonewall the iconic named queer bookstore, owned by the most adorable gay man. I sold my CDs there and got all my queer lit.

A few blocks further down the Street was Bottom's Up for a bit. A few blocks down the other way was where One in Ten opened. They were also a gay men's sex shop. CP was on Somerset Street. Two blocks over, on Lisgar Street, was Icon.

It truly was a small, gay village back then, and there were quite a few of us doing all this hopping through it daily. So many queers lived in Centretown, as well. It was great fun living and working downtown at the time. The queers owned the streets and we filled them regularly. Any apartments downtown would be quickly scooped up by queers. The village was ours, started and created by Brad and his dreams of making Ottawa what Toronto was—a gay haven.

When Brad died, it was a shock to all of us, me among the most. I hadn't seen him in a couple of years, and we'd had that falling out. His brother came and spent the three months Brad was ailing in hospital with him, and became my connection to Brad. That let us briefly reconnect, and allowed me to show him love while he was dying. When he passed away, the entire queer village took a massive hit.

It wasn't long before Donald realized he couldn't actually run the businesses without Brad. It was obvious to everyone, but it must have hit Donald hard. One at a time, over the next five years, each of the established and hugely successful queer businesses Brad had created and built up closed.

First it was Icon. Everyone was so shocked when they announced it was closing. It was right after the get-together for Brad's funeral on the main floor there. It was only a short while after that the entire place went up for sale. When it sold, it got refurbished into offices.

Next was CP. It went up for sale, but it took a few years before someone new took it over. The story was that Donald had made some deal with a regular bartender there that he would take over running it but it only took a few years until it lost its shine too. The queers stopped going. It closed, and the son of the buildings' owner took it over and made it into a new, non-gay bar.

Then, to everyone's surprise, Steamworks closed. That was the real signal that the heyday of our queer village of the nineties in Ottawa was over.

It wasn't long before Wilde's closed, and After Stonewall closed. Another gay bar tried to come in, owned by the same people who owned the Eagle's Nest, but eventually it closed, too. One in Ten shut down.

In the nineties, a huge portion of the queer community worked for the federal government. When they started making great money, many of them moved into houses in the suburbs of Ottawa. The big tech boom in Ottawa was also happening around the same period, and many folks were moving out to Kanata, the suburb where most of the major tech companies had set up shop.

Over the years, being queer has become more socially acceptable and condoned, people have gotten more educated, and we're so much more out of the closet now. As the city started to grow and create more suburbs, more queers moved into comfortable communities within those suburbs.

The party scene also shifted, from a time of heavy alcohol use more towards party drugs, like Ecstasy, that didn't need alcohol. Young people started only wanting water or energy drinks, and bars started losing money because alcohol sales were down. A great story told to me by a dear friend is that CP used to turn the cold water off in the washrooms, so you couldn't keep refilling your water bottle all night. I could totally see that happening.

Also, the times were changing, and as queers were finally becoming comfortable out in society, with little retribution, we started going to straight establishments and restaurants more.

Then the internet came, and shopping changed and buying changed, and hooking up and dating changed, and, well, everything changed.

It's true that the heyday of Centretown and the real gay village of Ottawa is now a thing of the past. Everything had closed, and everything was gone. Now when I go to Centretown to stop at a store or do any business around there, it's not the same feel at all. In fact, it's completely different.

It's not gay people on every corner like it once was. It's not a gay village. It makes me sad to see the banners that should have been erected twenty years ago, when so many queers went to so much trouble and effort to make it the village it was at the time. They belonged there then, not twenty years later, after everyone and everything was gone.

Ottawa's gay village in the nineties was a time and a place that I will forever be so proud to not only have experienced firsthand, but to have been deeply embedded in the culture of at the time. My big gay life. That's what it was for me, and for so many others.

～

By the mid-two thousands, the Centretown gay bars had all but for one or two disappeared. There was no better time to start a festival for queers where they could be in the spotlight right in the heart of the city.

That was my plan, and I had the festival chops now to do it, because of the Rock City Women's Fest. I needed to figure out a way to bring my queer festival downtown. It was a dream I'd been building for a while, the dream of queers on stage in the middle of the city. A city we were feeling more comfortable in every day.

26

BOW OUT AT BEEBLEBROX

After Brad died, I was still playing music with my band, Elaina and the Chain, but I wasn't happy. It hadn't been the same without Brad, and it wasn't fun anymore. Ken, my viola player who lived in the States, wasn't traveling up as much, because Ottawa had almost no gay bars and no downtown bathhouse anymore. Why would a gay man travel from the United States to come to a city with no gay culture?

I felt a deep need to quit. I woke up one day and did exactly that. I quit it all. We had been playing without Brad—myself singing lead; Janet on bass; Pete, a friend of Janet's on drums; and Geoff on guitar. We played in bars and the crowds would show up and scream for us, but I had lost my sparkle.

I lost that twinkle in my eye for playing music when Brad died. I tried to get it back, but it wouldn't come. I was always sad when I held the mic. I also wasn't close to anyone else in the band, and it was so cold up there without him. No one looked at me when I sang or played. I felt like they were all up there for themselves. And maybe they were.

I would think of Brad and our nights performing together, and about playing and the piano lounge and how the music I was making now was nowhere near the same level as when I was with Brad, a master pianist. Now it was rock and roll, and loud, and felt empty and meaningless to me. And I quit.

I called each of my band members as soon as I woke up and my decision was clear. I thought, "Why make them wait? I should just do it now." So I did.

I called up Janet first. We talked and I tried to explain to her that I was too sad and couldn't do it anymore, that it wasn't what I wanted. I needed to quit the band. And, since it was my band, Elaina and the Chain, I guess I was closing the band. Janet wasn't even listening to me. She was angry from the first words out of my mouth. She had become well known playing with me, and been given major opportunities playing with me and to her, I was now taking this all away.

I called Geoff, and Pete, the drummer, her friend who I'd never really felt all that great about to be honest. He was straight and just didn't fit to me. Janet should have known that, but we had needed a drummer and she put him in. I told Geoff and him the same things, that I was sad and couldn't do it anymore. They reacted the same way: they got mad. It was like I was taking something away from each of them. I felt like they were all being selfish.

I realize I sound biased here. It's been years since I've even mentioned this. It's no longer a big deal to me. But, at the time, all of their reactions broke my heart even more. I had been so good to them all. I'd included them in everything I was ever doing—the festivals, the gigs, the money, my recordings, all of it.

It turned out all the band members were mad at me. They blamed me for taking away their chance at stardom. They all believed I could make it, and that they'd be coming along with me. Maybe that could have happened. Maybe we were destined for it to happen. But no, it wasn't in the cards for me. I wasn't interested in playing this way anymore, it didn't feel good.

I also wasn't close to anyone in the band like I was with Brad. Well, I was with Ken, my viola player. In fact, twenty-plus years later, we still talk weekly. I've always had a loving and honest relationship with Ken. He always understood me. He also wasn't counting on me for stardom or anything like that. He was in it for the fun and experience of rocking out in a band after years of playing classical music. He was gay and sweet and charming and beautiful. After he started playing with us regularly, I gave him a key to my apartment, so he could stay on my couch rather than at Steamworks. Or do both; his choice. We spent a lot of intimate time both on stage and in my apartment.

I never had those bonding opportunities with the other band members. They would show up at practice or gigs and play, but we weren't connected on a personal level like Brad and Ken and I all were. To the others, it was a job, one they thought might make them eventually famous. And when I quit music, I took that from them.

I had felt disenchanted with performing for quite a while before that, but not for one second did any of them comfort me or ask me how I was doing. They didn't take note of the things right in front of their eyes, like the way Brad dying had obviously affected me.

I hung up after calling all of them, feeling even more defeated and sad. I got a phone call a few days later. It was a Dyke friend of mine, and she was calling to fill me in that Janet has started a new band called Unchained. I cried. I cried and cried so hard, for what felt like weeks.

The band started to get gigs at the places I had played before breaking up Elaina and the Chain. They called the venues I had booked us at previously, and promised a similar experience to what we had brought them. But then they'd flop and lose the spot.

The cycle continued for a while until no one would book them. The problem was, they didn't have a strong lead singer. It hurt me badly. I had been going through an immensely hard time and their response was this bizarre retaliation band. Unchained – as though I had them chained and their release from me was some form of liberation.

About a year after I broke up my band, I got a job near my place, doing marketing for a business. I got another call from a friend of mine. A local musician, Danielle, had a few bands at that time, and one of them had played at the Rock City Women's Fest. We had gotten to know each other a bit. She was an incredibly sweet woman, still is.

Danielle asked if I would open for her big show at Zaphod Beeblebrox. It was a CD release at the iconic Ottawa live music venue. The place had seen every Canadian act, from low-level amateurs merely starting up, to the highest level of singers and artists in our country. It was owned by an equally iconic man. Ottawa wouldn't have even had a spot on the map of Canadian music venues without him. At one point, he had two Beeblebrox Live music venues in the city.

I spent an hour on the phone with Danielle explaining what had happened recently with my former band. I was forlorn on the phone with her. She understood.

The next week, Danielle called me back and said she had a song for me. She then dropped it by my place for me to hear. I loved it. It was a friendship serenade, and the words spoke of power and patience and friendship. I loved Danny for it. It was so darn sweet of her to do that, and it helped my broken heart at the time. I called her back the next day from work and told her that, if she still needed an opener, I'd love to do it. I'd do it solo and make it my final Ottawa appearance. I felt I needed that. I told her I couldn't wait.

I hadn't played solo in a long time, not since D-Bar in Sudbury. I was scared and nervous. My new boss at the time came to watch my performance, as did my new friends from where I lived then.

The gay City of Ottawa councillor Shawn Little came, too. He lived in the same area I was living in, and was a colleague and friend of my boss. He also knew me from years before, at CP.

Some old Dyke friends came out, as well, and some gay men and a handful of people I was still in touch with from Rock City. It was a lovely night. I opened up my solo set with an original song, then continued to play all of my originals. I only played two covers that night: *Gold Dust Woman* by Stevie Nicks and *Joey* by Concrete Blonde, from two of my all-time favourite singers and albums.

The night was wonderful, with the most loving people in attendance. I played each song like it was my last, using as much of my vocal power and precision as I could. My new boss was very impressed. I hadn't mentioned I was singer when she'd interviewed and hired me, and I'd only been working with her for a year now. And I had been sore about it all. I'd wanted to start my new life, one where I didn't talk about my old one.

That's what I had done. I had started working with this straight woman, in a very straight area, with all these straight businesses, and I'd kept my head down and worked hard.

The entire time, though, I had also been planning, thinking, and dreaming. I wanted to bring Rock City into the light of day, to the light of the city, and to the many people who would be able to attend if it weren't so far away.

The night at Beeblebrox did turn out to be, essentially, my final performance. It would be many years before I would play to a public crowd again. I put my mic down and I let that part of my life disappear, while I honed my producer chops.

I wanted to make another festival.

Even though Rock City had not been the success financially that it should have been, it had been a great start at creating something powerful and important. It had provided a platform for queer artists—a safe, professional, caring, and open space for them to perform, and to be taken care of and uplifted.

It was great that I'd had time away from it, though. We couldn't pull together enough funding to keep it going, so it had to end. But, no longer playing, performing, and planning Rock City gave me great space to think.

I took two full years off from all of that before I got started with my next big idea. This time, I would bring my dream to the city, and the queers would play out in the open, out in public, not hidden away in a dimly lit cafe or nightclub, not once a year at Pride, and not out in a closed quarry in Wakefield.

27

OUT ON THE STREET

At my new job, I got to meet a lot of new people, including business folk from the area and political figures. I was hired to help the street I lived by attract customers. It was under construction, and we were making ad campaigns. I made a coupon book for the local businesses, and created all kinds of initiatives to bring people down there during that dusty time. I worked three days a week at that job, and i liked it.

I liked the woman who had hired me, and whom I worked with. It was just the two of us in the office, and she was cool. Most importantly, she was gay positive. I never hid who I was or who I was dating with her. She didn't like the word Dyke when I used it, which only made me use it more often, but everything else was a non-issue.

After Rock City was over, I ended up at home in an apartment with nothing to do. With me working three days a week, I spent the rest of my time walking my little Toni, my Chihuahua, through my neighbourhood daily, and talking to the locals. Toni and I would stop in at the shops and get to know people. It became a regular thing for us.

I became friends with a man who was dating a closeted lesbian and worked down the street from my new apartment. He had shown up with her to the last Rock City, since the second edition was open to everyone. He was so impressed with the event that he went back to the community we shared and told everyone how cool I was and what he had seen me pull off.

Anytime I'd walk into his shop now, he would brag about me. He ended up bragging to the business that ultimately hired me. They called me for an interview. I was so full of ideas and brainstormed so heavily with her during that first meeting, she hired me on the spot. I felt fantastic, like someone could see me and quickly recognize my fairly new, but honed, skillset.

I was hired to help with marketing and events. I was essentially doing everything I had done for Rock City, but shifted over to this street.

The City of Ottawa councillor for the area was Shawn Little. He was well known, because he was the wildest person on council by a long shot. The stories the paper would tell about him, looking back at it all, feel like they were all because he was gay. They picked on him because he was different. I think he got a hard time on council, and was never given a break, because of deep homophobia there.

I only wish Shawn, in his lifetime, could have experienced Mayor Jim Watson coming out as gay. But that would happen in 2019, more than ten years after Shawn's death. Today, there's also Catherine McKenny, an out nonbinary City of Ottawa councillor. Shawn would have been in perfect company now.

At Shawn's time, it was obvious council didn't treat Shawn with the respect he deserved. But, his constituency sure did. He was a great councillor and took care of a lot of crap in that neighbourhood during his time on council.

I got to know, Shawn quite well in those year. He was very sweet and kind, polite and earnest. That's why I wasn't surprised when I saw all the respect he was given in the local community. Everyone I ever met loved Shawn. At City Hall, though, it seemed like they were always trying to shame him and get rid of him.

Shawn and I had met each other years before at CP, so when he popped into my office with his assistant to speak to my boss, we were pleasantly reunited. It was amazing to see him, I had heard about the gay City of Ottawa councillor, but I hadn't ever met Shawn as a councillor. When he came into the office with his suit on, and I was introduced to him as Councillor Shawn Little, I was a bit shocked. He looked a lot different from the guy in the football jersey and track pants I was used to seeing at CP.

He came over to my desk and gave me the biggest hug. He introduced me to his assistant, whom I would become very good friends with. His name was Gabriel, and he was quite stylish. He was a French boy who could have been a model. He was also smart, friendly, gay positive—obviously—and funny. He wasn't gay at all, but I loved him instantly.

Gabriel sat down with me, while Shawn and my boss talked some city business, and we got to know each other a bit. I shared with him my plans to start a new festival, this time in the city, one where queer performers could be seen and experienced out in the open.

I explained how hard it was for queer artists to get ahead when we were always only performing in basement bars and nightclubs, or once a year at Pride. I wanted a more main street mainstream opportunity for queer performers. Gabriel loved the idea and told me to leave it with him.

A couple of days later, Gabriel called me and said that he'd talked my ideas over with Councillor Little. He said that, if I was serious, Shawn's office would do everything in their power to assist me. Well, that was that.

I spoke to my boss and we started to plan. I asked her if she could convince her board to put in some money, to help get me started. She got them to give me five thousand dollars for the first year. I was to raise the rest on my own.

Quite honestly, as I was talking to them all about it back then, and saw the way they'd look at me when I was explaining my ideas, I could tell they didn't fully understand what I was planning. They were all just pleased someone had ideas and wanted to do something, and they supported me in doing it. That was great and it gave me the encouragement I needed.

I started figuring out what and where the festival would be, and what I would need to pull it all off. I wanted the stage to be outside, and right on the street. And I wanted to fill the street with people. I wanted to put queers on stage, align them with a lineup of mainstream artists, and bring in a big headliner. That would surely draw crowds and give queer artists more of a profile locally.

Now, I just had to find all the money. Gabriel and Councillor Little took care of all of the City of Ottawa permits and allowances, which was a big load off of me, coming from private property, where I didn't have those issues. The city made you jump through so many hoops, and that was all new to me. Councillor Little ended up giving me Gabriel almost full time in the couple of months leading up to the first festival.

I thought long and hard and came up with a name. I liked shortening festival to fest; it felt cool. And, where I would be holding it would be just west of downtown Ottawa. So, I decided it would be called Westfest. Everyone loved the name right away.

I went from business to business with my one-pager about the event I was dreaming of, explaining how, by taking part, each business could raise their profile, draw people to them, and receive significant exposure at my event. They all jumped on board. The sponsorships were coming at me at a pace I wasn't accustomed to.

Raising money for Rock City had been like pulling teeth. No one was interested. I get it. It was far away, it was called a women's festival, it was in Quebec. There were all kinds of reasons for its demise. But this, this was different. It branded the area it was in, it was going to be out on the street, and it came with my promise to bring thousands of people to this street for it. That was very appealing to everyone.

The street had been partially closed to traffic due to the construction, and the shops were dead because of it. They were all very ready for something to help bring them people and sales. I promised this would be it. They were enthusiastic and fully on board.

Outside of Councillor Shawn Little and his incredible assistant, there was one other woman who helped me pull it all together, and supported me so much in that first year. Her name was Kerri. She was the manager of the Scotiabank on my street at the time. She was on the board of the business I worked for, as well. I met her at one of the board meetings when she came into our office. She was delightful, hilarious, pretty, and outgoing. We hit it off right away.

I asked Kerri if she could help me with my finances, now that I had a regular paycheque—a solid, same amount every two weeks. It was security for me, and something I hadn't had since I'd worked in corrections. It was time to deal with the fact that I had zero credit. Actually, I had bad credit, since the portable toilet company from Rock City had sued me when they didn't get their money after the second festival. They were the only service providers we couldn't pay. I couldn't help it; we didn't have it to give. They had brought me to court, and it had gone on my personal credit rating.

Kerri had me come into her office. She sat with me for over an hour that first visit. She talked me through everything, and said we could fix it all. We started planning. First, she was going to help me get that bad credit taken care of. We developed a plan to make payments to the debt company and, after a while, it was covered.

We also set out to get me my first-ever credit card, and that was an empowering feeling, too. Kerri helped me start saving money, which I had never been taught to do, and certainly never had done. I had always just been surviving and not saving for my future. I'm not sure I ever believed I had a future. For as long as I could remember, that wasn't the way my brain worked.

But now, Kerri was helping me plan for my future. She helped me get life insurance. She helped me buy my first home. And, she helped my festival get off the ground. She became one of my first directors on the board of the newly incorporated Westfest non-profit organization I created. She also gave us a ten-thousand dollar sponsorship cheque in our first year.

I would say Kerri was pivotal in my growth, and my successes. We're still good friends today. How could I not be friends with her? She was kind of like the mother I never had, but way funnier than I could have ever dreamed.

I got the local massive car lot to sponsor us. They put a big, new car on a lift right next to my stage that first year. The advertising was well worth the five thousand bucks for the festival, and the new car they gave me to drive for the duration, in exchange.

Everything was working incredibly well, and everyone I spoke to leapt onboard. It was truly shocking to me at the time, but so empowering. After years of me begging for support and not getting it, people were finally giving it to me. Hell, they were tracking me down to get involved.

I booked Jane Siberry, a Canadian icon, to headline the very first Westfest. Opening for her was a slew of local queer and mainstream artists. We particularly had a lot of female artists and Dykes.

It was time to get out of the closet. It was the right time in history to raise the ceiling and push the roof right off. It was time for queer people to get the exposure we deserved for our talents, and to take ownership of our space.

I had gathered tons of queer volunteers and locals to help with it all. It became a real, open, loving community of people running Westfest. My new festival was full of gay volunteers, artists, and musicians, out on the street in the middle of the city, and the crowd was full of queers.

The first event was one day long. That morning, while we were closing the street, putting up the stage, and barricading all over the place for public safety, I was floating. Gabriel and I were doing all this work, running around like chickens with our heads cut off, and we made it all happen. He was my copilot, for sure; he did everything. Hell, at one point he was chucking beers in the bar area, the next he'd be moving portable potties. He worked with sponsors for me. Gabriel did everything he could to help me, and so did Councillor Little.

Over five thousand people attended our stage in our first year, and Westfest was deemed a success by all. The *Ottawa Citizen* had lengthy articles about the excitement the event had generated, printing photos of Jane Sibbery, as did the *Ottawa Sun* and CBC, which had come on board as our media sponsor. Everyone was talking about Westfest.

We weren't hiding in basements anymore. We were now out in the middle of a city street in the nation's capital. And I was manifesting my dream of having queer artists treated right and get the exposure they deserved.

In laying down my mic and guitar I said goodbye to the world of performing and jumped backstage full time to make the music festival industry what I always dreamed it could be.

Years of hauling my own equipment and fussing over details like travel and food before hitting a stage taught me a lot about how to put on the best possible show.

I challenged myself to create an experience and an opportunity for queer artists, all artists really, that would be second to none, and we did. The reality in a lot of event production is that the artist is viewed as a service provider and only valued for their time on stage. Everything leading up to it is deemed as inconsequential. From personal experience, I know that the best show, comes from an artist who is well cared for. I would go to extra lengths to prioritize the experience and well-being of the artists who came to Westfest, and invariably, they returned that love to the audiences, tenfold.

A few years later, I met the love of my life, my Rowan. They are the best partner and relationship I've ever experienced. We shacked up and got kitties and puppies and plants, and started a garden, and life was joyous, and I continued to run my festival while they pursued their art practice and teaching career.

Our life has been lovingly awesome, and we've shared all of it together. We traveled a lot in the first couple of years, seeing places we had dreamed of seeing, making our own road trip memories.

Over the next five years, Westfest grew at an exponential rate. By the festival's fifth anniversary, we were closing and taking over ten city blocks of a main artery of Ottawa. Filling the streets and stages (there were multiple at this point) with performers of every possible expressive medium. There grew to be literary and spoken word showcases, dance performances of all kinds, performance artists, circus acts, sports demonstrations, drag queens…

That's not all, though. I made it a personal thing for me to always have as many of the openers for the headliners as possible be locals, and to get them as much press exposure as I could. That was huge for so many local bands and artists at the time in Ottawa as there was a perception that to gain any musical credential one had to leave the city in order to be able to come back and access the larger festivals.

I wasn't as embedded in queer culture as I had been in my earlier life, and I certainly was working and dealing with a lot of straight people, comparatively but my unabashed and overt queerness helped, in many ways, empower and show straight allies how to find ways to support queer artists. I missed being embedded in a small localized queer community neigborhood and being right smack-dab in the middle of it, but I had made a small community with this festival and its ever growing support team of volunteers and crew.

And, the queers certainly all came to Westfest. The street each year would be full of queers and their children and dogs walking around, taking in the sights, scenes and entertainment the sprawling festival had to offer. They felt free and comfortable and invited. They knew a big Dyke was running the show. They knew of me, and they knew I'd have a safe space for them all.

Working my way from one end of the festival, down the city blocks, to the other end on my golf cart, I would meet all kinds of old friends as I popped from scene to scene, ensuring everything was going smoothly. I had queer musicians taking part on the multiple stages, queer crew and volunteers making it all run smoothly, queer artists of every creative expression animating the streets, all of us playing our parts and working at my different festival bars and side events. So, ultimately, I did have a big queer family; it was just extended, now, into mainstream life. Which was what I had always wanted, right?

ACKNOWLEDGMENTS

This memoir was possible to write because of the love and support, editing and advice of my brilliant Cara Tierney.

Thanks to my talented, and gentle Editor, Anita Dolman.

Special thanks to Bill Staubi for being the single biggest supporter of Queers in Ottawa making him my hero, but also my generous Beta Reader and constant cheerleader.

Thank you to my other two encouraging Beta Readers and long-time dear friends Marti Carding, and Melissa (Milly) Keeping, I love you.

Special thanks to the most talented Graphic Designer Lisa Georges, for jumping in to design the covers for this series so generously.

I am more grateful than I can express to the following people for being in my corner, thank you; Debbie Owusu-Akyeeah, Bill Tierney, Deborah Campbell, Samantha Wiengarten, Desiree Lefebvre, Sly Lefebvre, Thomas Dempsey, April O'Brien, Sharon Ash, Kim

Cairns, my brother Mike Lewandowski, my nisîmis Tessa Cook, Candyrose Freeman, and Jacques Pompon Minoune Bourdeau.

Also, to the many generous people who purchased and supported my first book, DYKE, a memoir. To those who sent emails and messages to me opening up about your own intimate life details and struggles, thank you, you inspire me so much.

A beautiful byproduct of me writing my memoirs has been all the people i've reconnected with to confirm details for these books. This part of the process has been very special.

I feel I would be remiss if I didn't at some point, in this book, make mention of the fact that the entire world is living, coping and trying hard to survive during, the COVID 19 coronavirus pandemic. It is now October 2020 and this disease has already killed and affected hundreds of thousands of people world-wide. I'm thankful and privileged to be hiding in the woods, safely, writing, while many others must sacrifice daily, to provide essential and necessary services for everyone. I salute all of you and I thank you deeply. I hope for a safe and better future for all the young people who have yet to live their lives fully and I dream for a safe, healthy, vibrant and prosperous future for them.

ABOUT THE AUTHOR

Elaina Martin is a Canadian, butch Dyke singer, songwriter, and author, and writes fiction and non-fiction. She recorded the EP *Cancer Woman* in 2000. She is an award-winning live event producer and director. In 2001, her short story "The Homecoming" appeared in *Hot & Bothered 3: Short Short Fiction on Lesbian Desire* (Arsenal Pulp Press). In June 2020, she released her first book in the three-book Dyke series to glowing reviews. Martin lives a proud queer life with her partner, Cara Tierney.